LAST SEEN ONLINE

By Tapzac

Last Seen Online

Gossip Travels Faster than Wi-Fi

ISBN: 978-93-343-7403-2

First Edition: 2025
For permissions, contact: tapzac123@gmail.com

To all whose love language

is gossip

TABLE OF CONTENTS:

Chapter 00: *GTA Five Star behavior*

Chapter 01: *Welcome To the Jungle*

Chapter 02: *Ex and the City*

Chapter 03: *See you Latte*

Chapter 04: *Infamous Last Words*

Chapter 05: *The Unusual suspects*

Chapter 06: *For your FYI only*

Chapter 07: *Hiring for the position of "murderer"*

Chapter 08: *The Devil Wears Timepieces*

Chapter 09: *To CC or Not to CC*

Chapter 10: Finger Guns and Roses

Chapter 11: *The whole truth and nothing but the truth*

Chapter 12: *Show off must go on*

Chapter 00

GTA FIVE STAR BEHAVIOR

The office runs on three things: caffeine, incompetence, and gossip. You'd think it's work, but no. The work is just background noise for the real game — who's hooking up, who's breaking down, and who's about to rage-quit after that "friendly feedback" call.

Politics? Oh, please. This place has more strategic alliances than the parliament. I once saw a guy give someone a shoutout in a meeting just so they wouldn't rat him out for coming in two hours late. HR called it "cross-functional appreciation." I call it "*blackmail with benefits*".

You think promotions are about talent? LOL. Promotions are awarded to whoever makes the least noise and the most colourful PPTs. If you're actually good at your job, you're punished by being made the "go-to" person — aka unpaid tech support with a fancy title.

And don't even get me started on the whisper networks. There are more theories flying around than in a true crime subreddit. Sam once complimented someone's profile picture, and suddenly there was a full-blown rumour he was engaged to three women in three cities.

And now Sonia's dead. And everyone's either too shocked to speak or too busy updating their LinkedIn headers to "Empathetic Leader. Mental Health Ally."

Covid didn't just hit — it guillotined normal life. And in the chaos, the working world discovered its second-greatest invention after paid time off: "work from home." Sure, it has perks—where else can you attend meetings from kitchen watching Sherlock reruns in shorts But honestly, the hardest part was being socially distanced from my girlfriend, Reya, who—full disclosure—was the only reason I joined this corporate circus in the first place.

But just when cabin fever was starting to feel romantic, things took a turn. One of our colleagues took the concept of "involuntary leave" very literally and apparently "off-ed" herself. that too a day before the deadline, no less! The sheer audacity to die before finishing their work. Truly, some people will do anything to avoid a Monday.

Now all we can do is sit around debating: Do we work for a company with a secret serial killer or where people would rather die than join another one on one with the manager, or do we all subconsciously hate this place enough to volunteer as tribute? One thing's certain: Reya won't let me die before she has the chance to marry me (clearly, she wants all my paid leave to herself). Until our corporate wedding, she keeps me alive and entertained—my Sherlock sidekick in mapping all the office gossip, debunking rumours and for some dark reason, making me wear sunscreen even though my only exposure is to the blue light of my laptop at this time of lockdown.

If the world ends, at least HR will have a killer attendance record.

I never fancied myself a writer—hell, calling me a reader would be a cosmic joke. Unless you count the novels I skimmed under duress or Textbooks I half-read to pass exams I barely cleared. I'm more of a movie guy. Give me murder mysteries, true crime, broody detectives, and Sherlock marathons—I've watched enough to suspect my neighbour's cat of tax evasion.

So, when scandal strikes at the office—an affair here, an arrest there, maybe a thrilling "was it really suicide?" scenario—deadlines don't just slip, they vanish into witness protection. Suddenly, I'm less "employee of the month" and more "detective on the scene." Was it murder? Suicide? Or worst, just a rumour?

Either way, I've got popcorn, a notepad, and just enough screen-induced insomnia to solve this office mystery—or at least write a book compiled of all the chats, emails related to the "case" that can be useful to police or reason of my suspension to HR. Only time will tell.

Subject: Digital Evidence Submission – Regarding Sonia Arora.

From: Neil V. Mehta <neil.mehta@nurobitsolutions.com>

To: Cybercrime Unit, Mumbai Police

Date: 19th oct 2025

Dear Officers,

What follows is a compilation of internal chats, emails, and metadata from our digital workplace at Nurobit Solutions, submitted in connection with the death of my colleague, Sonia Arora. As well as the analysis that led me to suspect Sonia's death wasn't what it seemed. Think of this as my attempt at Sherlock Holmes meets cybersecurity best practices (minus the nicotine addiction, plus the metadata).

The official conclusion was suicide. But something about it never sat right. There was always something more to it and I think I figured it out. I am not a detective, I mostly code as a professional and watch way too many murder mystery documentaries but I do think I found the something that makes it impossible to stay quiet. My hope? That the information here provides your investigation with exactly what it needs. At the very least, it's a pretty gripping read.

Kind regards,
Neil V. Mehta
Remote Automation Consultant
Nurobit Solutions

Nurobit Solutions - India Office Hierarchy

- **Mr. Kapoor** — Head of deliveries - India ("Self made" business man with a rich dad)
  - **CJ** — Designated HR (Head of rumours and policies)
  - **Dev** — Tech & Infrastructure Lead (Workaholic tech daddy)
    - **Vik** — IT Security (manager of mysterious logins)
    - **Neil** — AI Automation Consultant (head of dark humour & nhilism division)
    - **Aerron** — Sr. Software Developer (Tech God, Gym Rat, caffeine abuser")
    - **Sonia** — UI/UX Developer (Flirts with danger and deadline)
    - **Sahil** — Back-End Developer (CEO of uncomfortable silence)
    - **Ritika** — Back-End Developer (PPT philosopher and definitely "fun at parties")
    - **Rishab** — Intern (eye contact avoider)
  - **Anya** — Head of marketing I guess (CEO's daughter, knows nothing, does nothing)
  - **Sid** — Strategy & Content Lead (Creepy genius with a God complex)
    - **Dia** — Sr. Data Analyst (gender swapped Steve Jobs without talent and..cancer)
    - **Reya** — Sr. Graphic Designer (Design Goddess. Therapist. Human Lie Detector)
    - **Amaan** — Jr. Graphic Designer (Has trauma from accidentally replying all.)
    - **Sam** — Sr. front-End Developer) (Creative consultant for moral grey zones)
    - **Maya** — Jr. Strategist (Sr. Boundary tester)
    - **Mini** — literally no idea what she does (exists)

Jay — Newbie (Walking Red Flag with a British Accent.)

Chapter 01

WELCOME TO THE JUNGLE

[Microsoft Teams – #design-strategy – 09:09 AM]

CJ: Good morning, team. Please fill out the quarterly corporate engagement self-assessment form by EOD today. Yes, that's a real thing. No, I didn't make it up.

Also, please welcome our new team member, Jay Malhotra. He joins us with a master's degree from the UK and extensive international experience. We're excited to have him on board.

Dev: Welcome aboard, Jay. I'm Dev, heading front-end strategy. My partner-in-suffering, Sid, leads back-end architecture.

Sid: Hi Jay, welcome welcome. I have a boring coding experience, but I lead a colourful team with interesting people. I'll let the team introduce themselves.

Maya: Welcome, Jay! I work as a Junior Strategist. Currently in a situationship with Excel. It's toxic but efficient.

Dia: Welcome! happy to see a familiar face, I think you were my jr. during my time in UK.

I work as a Senior Data Analyst here btw.

Neil: Welcome, Jay. I am a Tech Consultant. Remote. Mysterious.

Sonia: welcome. I'm a UX Designer.

Amaan: Welcome to the madness jay, I'm a graphic designer.

Nikita: Hi Jay, welcome aboard! QA/Test engineer here.

Reya: Welcome Jay, Senior Graphic Designer here. Fluent in fonts, gossips.

Sahil: Welcome Jay, coder here, all the best!

Ritika: Welcome Jay! I'm backend developer as well.

Vik: IT Security. I see everything. I say nothing.

Mini: Welcome, Jay! Hope you're ready for terrible coffee and terrific deadlines.

Aerron: Welcome Jay! I'll be five minutes late, gym went long.

Rishab: Welcome jay

Jay: Hi all, thanks for the welcome. Excited to be here! Hoping to learn, collaborate, and good to see you too Dia.

CJ: Also, belated happy birthday to Neil Mehta! Hope you had a relaxing weekend. Don't forget to log that cake slice in your timesheet 😉

Neil: Thanks, CJ! Appreciate the last on agenda wishes.

Mini: Happy belated, Neil!

Amaan: Happy birthday, bossman.

Reya: You turned a year older and still haven't aged a day, Mr. Mysterious.

Neil: That's moisturizer and unresolved trauma, thank you very much.

Dev: Also, shoutout to Neil and Aerron for their help with the pitch last week. Clients happy.

Neil, any update on the backend for the AI Assistant?

Neil: Almost there—just need Aerron to help iron out a few things.

Dev: He's working with me today and tomorrow.

Meanwhile, can you start working on the UI with Sonia?

Neil: Got it. Sonia, ready to suffer together?

Sonia: Aren't we always?

(Private Teams Chat – Neil <> Sonia - 10:34 AM)

Neil: Front-end UI hell, here we come.

Sonia: Remote boy finally enters the battlefield.

When are you flying to Mumbai? Your office *and* your girlfriend are here.

Neil: When COVID cases stop multiplying like bacteria.

So... sometime before the next apocalypse/year.

Neil: Also, how dare you not wish me a happy birthday?

Sonia: OMG I wrote you a handwritten letter with a wax seal and everything.

Must've forgotten to post it.

Neil: Lies.

Our generation doesn't even know where to *buy* stamps.

Sonia: Fine, happy belated birthday.

You don't look a day over six. Emotionally.

Neil: I'll take it.

Neil: Hey. You were oddly formal in the chat. You, okay?

Sonia: Yeah... just. Jay.

Neil: Jay Malhotra? New guy Jay?

Sonia: Yep. My ex. From a few years ago.

Neil: Oh damn. Like ex-ex?

Sonia: Ex with issues. Violent. Possessive. Controlling.

Not the good kind of crazy.

Neil: Well, that explains the cold welcome. You never forget your first and you never forget your worst.

Sonia: just—don't mention I told you. I didn't even tell Dia or Sam. And speaking of Sam... he's been weird lately.

Neil: wow Sam the flirt is weird, also in other news water found to be wet.

Sonia: Flirty? bro says can I ask a question related to the project and the straight up asks Personal questions.

Long stares. I don't know.

He's engaged, right?

Neil: Yep. To that data analyst from Pune.

Been together since college, I think.

Sonia: Ugh. That's what's messing with me.

I'm already seeing someone outside work. No drama wanted.

Neil: Do I get three guesses?

Sonia: You get zero. I'm trying to keep this clean.

Neil: Irony level: Office. Chat. Drama.

Sonia: 🙃

Neil: You okay though? With Jay being around?

Sonia: Yeah. Just need to focus. And ignore the ghosts.

Neil: That explains the cold welcome.

You never forget your first and you never forget your worst.

Sonia: unfortunately, yess, now to the project...

(We went on to discuss the project—something utterly irrelevant to why Sonia ended her story early. Sure, you could argue the work was soul-crushingly dull, enough to drive anyone to the edge. But here's the real kicker: Sonia actually loved her job and was damn good at it. So if anyone around here deserves to off themselves over work, it's definitely HR)

(Private WhatsApp Chat – Neil <> Reya – 2:03PM)

Reya: I swear, if HR emails me one more "self-assessment" forms I'm going to list "Faking enthusiasm for pointless paperwork" as my only skill.

Oh, cool, let's all rank our synergy on a scale of "Who cares" to "Why am I still alive?" That'll definitely boost productivity, right?

Neil: Babe.

You will NOT believe what Sonia told me today.

Reya: Hit me with it. I'm steeped and ready. Just finished telling HR my biggest weakness is not laughing in their face.

Neil: Sonia's ex just joined the team. Jay.

The "international experience" guy.

Reya: *Noooo.* That Jay?

Neil: Apparently he was psycho levels of controlling.

Now he's all "Great to be here 😁".

Reya: So she was cold for a reason.

Neil: Yup. You noticed too right, didn't even tell Dia or Sam. Told *me* though.

Reya: She trusts you. I like that.

But Dia is her best friend, she literally acts like her older sister, weird of her telling you and not her.

And let's keep "I can't talk without flirting" Sam out of any sentences that includes the word "trust".

Neil: Sam's been acting weird around her too. Flirty. Stares. Vibes.

Reya: Eww. Mr. Engaged needs to get a reality check! I fear Sonia has been single for so long that Sam might actually get lucky!

Neil: Sonia says she's already dating someone outside work.

Reya: Plot thickens. She complimented me twice today about my presentation but didn't mention any guy in her life, I think I need more coffee breaks with the girlies.

Anywayy who do we think?

Neil: No clue.

She shut me down before I could even guess.

Reya: Classic move. That means it's someone messier than a racoon at a buffet.

It's always the secret boyfriend with the soft launch and the red flags.

Probably someone from our office, probably her team mate, probably Sid.

Neil: Wow Sherlock, but she said he isn't' from the office and Sid is married with a kid too.

Reya: As if that would stop him, I saw him in the office getting weird when his phone rings, giggling and texting and then hiding the name, Tho my eagle eye saw it ...Bean Queen.

Neil: And you think this Bean Queen is not his wife.

Reya: Noop, married man in the office only smiles at a text on their phone either when their salary is credited or when their mistress texts them.

Neil: Entire office is one giant HR violation waiting to happen.

Reya: Agree to agree.

[Microsoft Teams – Dev:lopers (Dev, Aerron, Neil)– 05:16 AM]

Dev: Sorry to drop this at the last minute, but one of you heroic souls needs to handle Sam's deadline for me today.

I'm flying out to meet my girlfriend because her birthday trumps project management, and I trust you two not to turn my email into a resignation letter. It can't be Sam—guy's more likely to attach a meme with the deliverable.

Aerron: I've got a blood test and a full body systems diagnostic scheduled for my upcoming weightlifting competition but I'll jump in after the vampires finish with me.

Neil: Chill—heal up from that 2L blood loss, I got this.

Quick query though: why isn't Sid's own suicide squad helping? Isn't Sam their "problem child"?

Aerron: Happy to tag in later, but yeah, feels like Sid could at least pretend to manage his own team.

Dev: Sam blew it, and if Sid finds out, it might mess up his chances of upcoming promotions. That's why Sam dumped it on me... and now, lucky you.

Aerron: Still wild to me that you're buddies with Sam—his fiancée would probably ghost him if she saw the way he flirts with every moving object during billable hours.

Neil: Sonia told me he only asks about "deliverables" so he can segue into asking people their favorite color or deepest secret.

Aerron: why does he do that even tho he knows that everyone knows he is engaged.

Neil: Its like watching a snoman trying to get a sunbath.

Dev: Can we save the roast for after I escape Mumbai airspace? Forwarding the emails—just double-check the files before you fire off my digital signature into the void.

Neil: Yes, Captain. Also, your "urgent" flight is at night. That's, like, twelve power naps away.

Aerron: Bro, check the time on that sentimental watch we gave you on your birthday—unless you alleged "packing" is just you planning ways not to forget it.

Dev: That watch is my prized possession. Priorities: see girlfriend, look fly, owe you guys one universe-sized favor. Gotta pack—wish me luck.

Neil: Philosophers have long pondered: what does a man actually pack for one day in a different city with a lover? Is it hope? Suspense? Enough AXE to fumigate Bangalore and make it almost Delhi?

Aerron: One spare shirt, half a dozen underpants, and a prayer she doesn't dump him for overpacking.

Neil: Bro you are meeting the wrong lovers.

Aerron: That's how we minimalist roll!

Neil: 6 Underwear for one night is definitely not minimalism, she'll probably dump. Women can do anything!

Aerron: Why may I ask?

Neil: Strong independent woman can do anything, except leaving her career to be an housewife for her husband.

Aerron: I think women should be so independent they find their own G spot. Cuts down on disappointment for everyone.

Neil: Yeah that's another thing for philosophers to ponder.

(You know, the bond between us three is the only reason I survive this job. Dev is a genius coder, a firebrand leader, and a man so loyal he makes Romeo look lazy. Aerron, for all his extra years and medical mysteries, is basically my evil twin with better cholesterol. And here's the dark truth: I joined this firm for my girlfriend, but—shameless confession—after Covid, the first thing I'm excited about isn't seeing her, it's clocking in next to these two. Does that make me a bad boyfriend? No. It makes me a fantastic human, just catastrophically mediocre at romance. That's what sick leave is for.)

[Private WhatsApp Chat – Neil <> Reya - 10:49 PM]

Reya: You busy, Mr. Mysterious?

Neil: Just finished sending the client handover. Missed you. And at least two meals.

Reya: Aww. Want me to order your favourite burger?

Neil: Only if you include a side of you. 😩

Reya: We're doing bad pickup lines tonight? Cool.

Congrats again on the submission though — if you and Aerron don't get promoted in the upcoming promotions, I swear I'm launching a polite HR-approved rebellion.

Neil: "Respectfully, we riot". As long as there's chai at the sit-in, I'm in.

Reya: Speaking of tea...Jay Malhotra. The new guy. Dia says they were at the same uni in the UK. But she's not impressed. Claims he's all talk, no talent.

Neil: Bold claim. Man walks like he invented JavaScript.

Reya: I mean, he *looks* smart.

Like he moisturizes and looks people in the eyes when talking to them.

Neil: Maybe she liked him, and he ghosted her. Or worse... explained blockchain to her.

And what do you mean he "looks" smart? Doesn't he have masters degree from London?

Reya: LOL. As if a degree is the measure of brilliance.

Neil: no, it's a measure of temperature.

Reya: *Shut. Up.* The dude said he is a cinephile during lunch and guess what's his favourite movie is?

Neil: he is a bro so its either Shawshank redemption or the Fight club

Reya: guess more bro-er than that. His fav is fast and the furious. Anything after that he said was just noise to me.

Neil: Wow dude has no redeeming quality whatso ever. Don't get me wrong fast and furious are cinema to me as well but I won't consider it my fav.

Reya: if you don't have a fav just say any one of the Dune movies and move on, Shawshank is overrated now and shh, nobody talks about the fight club also Fast and furious is cinema" please don't say this in public if you ever want to be associated with me in the future.

Neil: what are you talking about they went to space; they're going to drive so fast (and furious) in the next one that they are going to travel thru time!

Reya: Oh god tell me it's not real.

Neil: they are calling it *"The Past & The Furious"*

Reya: God! Even I'm fast and curious now!

(Reya is terrifyingly good at everything. She'll design a flawless campaign in Figma, brew perfect chai, and psychoanalyze your childhood trauma before lunch—while wearing an oversized hoodie and calling you cute in three emotional tones.

She speaks Hindi, English, and sarcasm in the same sentence. I once spent an hour picking a font for a title (Bauhaus); she finished the pitch deck and changed the font while I wasn't looking.

She's emotionally intelligent, wildly talented, and knows when you're lying before you open your mouth. Once, I tried to hide feeling off—she sent a playlist, a meme, and a calendar invite for a "mental breakdown" at 9:30 PM, with 30 minutes blocked after for "Post-Crisis Snuggles."

Talking to her at the end of the day is the reboot. After a shift of pretending to care about Jira tickets and Dev's emotional baggage, her "You alive?" text restores my sanity.

She packages gossip, overthinking, and existential dread into a judgment-free zone—then roasts me, sends a cat meme, and says she loves me. In that order.

And here's the twist: I don't deserve her. I'm just the guy who wrote a Python script to order samosas faster. She's out here building brands, healing trauma, and holding this team together. But somehow, she picked me. As long as she keeps replying to my rants with "Call me, idiot," I'll be fine.)

How Work Gets Done at Nurobit Solutions

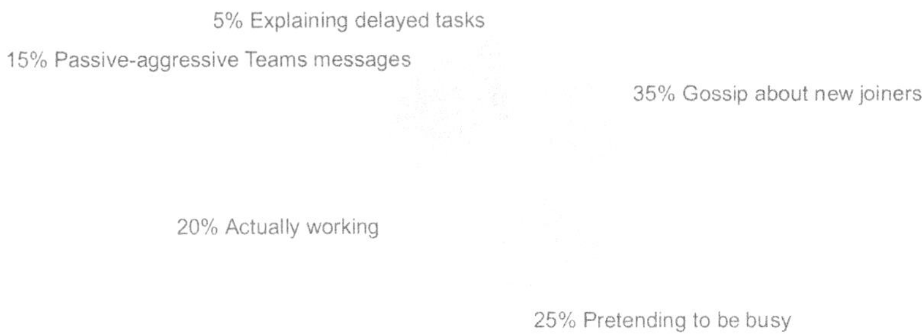

CHAPTER 02

EX AND THE CITY

[Microsoft Teams – #design-strategy – 09:02 AM]

CJ: Good morning, team. Reminder: today is the last day to submit your Q3 peer feedback forms. You know the drill: pretend at least reply to these reminders.

Dev: Thanks for the reminder, CJ.

Sid: Good morning, all.

Ritika: Morning!

Neil: Morning

Sahil: Guten Morgen!

Rishab: Godd Morning

Dia: Morning team ☀️

VIK: Top of the morning to everyone except whoever scheduled a 9 AM bug review.

Maya: Good morning! Also, my laptop finally updated after 4 restarts. So, I'm feeling dangerous.

Aerron: Morning, folks.

Sonia: morning

Jay: Morning, team. Excited to start contributing.

Amaan: morning morning ☕

Reya: morning! and good luck with your feedback therapy session

Dev: Sonia and Sid, please sync up on the Fintech Dashboard module today. Sonia, your wireframe doc from last week was on point.

Sonia: Thanks. Will connect with Sid post-meeting.

Sid: Sure. Let's aim for 12:30?

Sonia: works.

CJ: Side note: This Friday is the virtual team trivia night. Theme: "Nurobit Through the Ages." Yes, this is my legacy.

Neil: I have exactly 3 neurons left and one of them is holding onto weekend plans. Do we get lifelines?

CJ: Only if you agree to use your sick leaves.

(You know how every office has that one guy who somehow runs on Outlook reminders, black coffee, and the faint scent of hand sanitizer? Ours is CJ—our beloved HR rep, full-time policy parrot, part-time grief counsellor, and possibly a retired CIA operative based on how fast he redacts things.

CJ is... relentless. The man once onboarded an intern while he had dengue. Over Teams. With emojis. He smiled through a haemorrhagic fever, bro. I've seen him handle layoffs, theft allegations, a potential exorcism in the server room (don't ask), —all with the same tone he uses to wish people happy birthday. Polite. Optimistic. Dead in the eyes.

I genuinely believe CJ once sold his soul to Mephisto for a lifetime supply of corporate enthusiasm and exact change in the vending machine. In return, he became the perfect HR being—completely devoid of emotion, except when forwarding mental health webinar invites during a company crisis. He's the type who'd fire you with a smile and ask you to leave a Glassdoor review.

But—and this is important—he always tries to help. Like, genuinely tries. Need your PF transferred? He's there. Mental breakdown at 4 PM? He'll CC a wellness coach faster than you can say "burnout." Of course, once I started asking around, I learned things. Dark things. Like how CJ "accidentally" marked Dev's bereavement leave as optional volunteering hours. Or how he made a guy named Rishi attend an offboarding Zoom call... from his hospital bed. The man had appendicitis. CJ just said "the calendar invite was already sent."

And yet, despite all that, I can't hate him. Maybe it's the way he signs every email with "Warm regards" during summers and "Warmer regards" in the winter. Maybe it's because no one else would bother remembering everyone's work anniversary and blood group. Maybe it's because deep down, I know that in a world where HR is often a faceless arm of legal, CJ is... our faceless arm of legal, but with a smiley face sticker on it.

(Private Teams Chat – Neil <> Sonia - 12:42 PM)

Neil: Quick question, why exactly are you being punished with Sid?

Sonia: Because my Mercury is now in lemonade.

Neil: Damn. I knew astrology would eventually come for you.

Sonia: Also, because Dev is ducking that module and Sid begged for help. Dev owes me a coffee.

Neil: Yeah Dev is visiting his girlfriend in another city for her "belated birthday"

Sonia: LOL. That's what he told you?

Neil: You mean it like it's a lie. What do you know that I don't know.

Sonia: I don't know dude, he is your team lead and a friend, you must know.

Neil: Then he is out having the time of his life IF his GF forgives him! Idk how to recover from that, man must have to propose I guess.

Sonia: LOL. That seems like over exaggeration.

Neil: You say it like you don't believe in forgetting a birthday is a cardinal sin.

Sonia: its just a bday, get over it dude, they'll get you next year.

Neil: what's with you and bdays man, should I ask Jay?

Sonia: Trust me bro, you're better off not talking to him alsooooo, I recently found out he's divorced. Apparently, his wife left him last year.

Neil: Oof. Was he... like that with her too?

Sonia: That's the assumption. I only heard bits. He never hit me, but he had anger issues. And control. And walls punched. You get the vibe.

Neil: That makes me want to change all my passwords on your behalf.

Sonia: Appreciate it. I just want to ignore him and keep my head down.

Neil: Done. I'll pretend like I didn't hear the most dramatic backstory of 2020.

Sonia: LOL

(Sonia is brilliant in a way that isn't always convenient. She's not exactly close to me—we're more like those coworkers who orbit each other's lives without really colliding—but she's one of the few people here who gets my movie and Vine references without asking for context. Sometimes she even throws one back, deadpan, like she's been storing it for months. And occasionally, she'll do something wildly unexpected, purely, I suspect, for the plot.

I don't know her personally, not really. But I do know one thing: Sonia is damn good at her job. Stubborn as hell, never backs down, and will defend her designs like they're her children. She doesn't care for authority unless she respects it. Doesn't respond to messages unless they have a purpose. And if you ask her something dumb—like if she can "make the design more fun" without any context—she either ignores you or sends back an eerily specific three-page PDF explaining why you don't deserve a designer.

Beneath that fire-and-ice façade, she has this annoying tendency to be right. About people. About product flaws. About

Sam being a walking HR violation before anyone else notices. She can clock your mental state from your Slack typing speed. Once, she tells me I need a break before I even realize I'm burning out. "Your jokes are getting weird," she says. "Take a nap or quit."

She's the kind of person who leaves an impression—usually in the form of a carefully worded insult, a brilliant prototype, or a mysteriously deleted message that makes everyone suspicious.

(Private Teams Chat – Neil <> Vik - 3:08 PM)

Neil: Hey man, you ever get that VPN thing resolved.

Vik: Yeah, turns out it was just the firewall being melodramatic.

Neil: LMAO. Same energy as HR's fun Friday invite.

Vik: Don't remind me. CJ sent a calendar blocker titled "fun with the family."

Neil: We are the family now.

Vik: Stockholm syndrome but make it corporate.

Neil: 😂 Anyway, let me know if you need help setting up the new build. UI is... a journey.

Vik: Will ping you. And hey—if anything's acting sus on Sonia's system, let me know. Been patching some weird lag spikes.

Neil: All good so far. But yeah, will do.

(Vik, our IT guy, isn't a man so much as a presence—lurking between server fans and network cables, summoned only by "VPN not working" or "I forgot my password," which for me is every Monday.

He has one emotion: mild irritation. Communicates in grunts, ticket numbers, and sighs you can hear through chat. Asking for help once got me the reply: "Define help."

He drinks black coffee from a flask, codes in the dark, and demands cable ties as tribute if you enter his lair. I thought he was just a harmless wire-wizard—until I learned he's recovered deleted chat logs to win gossip wars, knows who failed phishing tests, and never forgets.

Terrifying, brilliant—built a firewall mid-migraine during a breakup. Not friendly, not blinky, but in a sea of shady emails and dodgy macros, he's the only thing between us and digital doom.)

(WhatsApp Chat – Neil <> Reya - 10:44 PM)

Reya: hii, you up so late

Neil: yeah, just sent the code push. missed you. Please take a flight and come here.

Reya: done. also, do you think Jay is full of crap or just... clueless?

Neil: bit of both? he said "I'm a team player" three times today like it was a self-talk before backing out of an ISIS mission.

Reya: Dia's not buying it. She rolled her eyes when he mentioned the UK

Neil: maybe because she knew him there and wasn't a fan?

Reya: I asked. She said "unfortunately." So.. yeah.

Neil: Poor Sonia. She seemed... off today.

Reya: yeah. didn't even reply to Maya in the girl's chat. Dia asked if she needs her anxiety pill but she said she would prefer cyanide.

Neil: maybe work pressure. She said Sid begged for help on that dashboard thing.

Reya: Sid gives me beige flag vibes.

Neil: Beige? Not red?

Reya: Reds too dramatic. He's more like... a tap that drips but never gets fixed

Neil: That's the best thing I've heard all day.

Reya: good. now sleep. I'll text you tomorrow after team chaos

Neil: night, my complete package of niceness

Reya: and you're my package of great compromises.

(You know, when all this started, I thought my biggest threat at work was death by boredom or maybe the wobbly ceiling fan in my room will take me out. Life was full of ridiculous tiny dramas—fighting with the landlord, surviving HR's personality quizzes, swapping existential memes with the guys, and wondering if Dev's long-distance girlfriend was just code for "solving Lee code problems alone."

But then, as if the universe got bored of watching us fill out self-assessment forms, reality dropped a plot twist so heavy even HR couldn't bury it in policy updates. Suddenly, the jokes weren't just about who microwaved fish or who'd survive the next round of layoffs. Suddenly, it got... serious. And I realized life isn't all team banter and cleverly named WhatsApp groups—sometimes, it's trying to figure out which one of your colleagues is hiding a killer instinct behind those awkward "reply all's.

But here's the thing: this isn't about office politics or who's best at pretending to like their manager's vacation pics. It's about finding out who did it—and, almost more importantly, why. And in this office, trust me, everyone's got a motive. Even the ceiling fans)

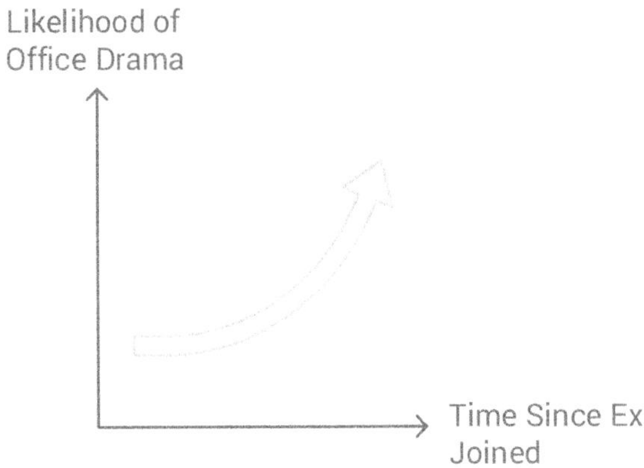

Likelihood of Office Drama over Time Since Ex Joined

Chapter 03

SEE YOU LATTE

[Microsoft Teams – #design-strategy – 09:36 AM]

Dev: Morning, all. Sid, you'll be leading the Fintech integration sprint today. Sonia, please sync with him and support where needed.

Sid: Got it. Sonia, let's connect at 11?

Sonia: morning, Sure.

Sahil: Morning. Just got my coffee. Ready to pretend I know what I'm doing.

Neil: Morning.

Vik: Mood.

Neil: Morning.

Maya: Morning everyone!

Dia: Morning guys.

Jay: Good morning team!

Amaan: Morning team

Ritika: Hi all, good morning!

Reya: Good morning.

Mini: Hi!

CJ: Good morning, team. No announcements today..

Neil: Suspicious. What's the catch?

CJ: The catch is your pending peer feedback, Mr. Mehta. 😉

Neil: Blocked and reported.

(Private Teams Chat – Neil <> Sonia - 12:19 PM)

Neil: You alive? need you help for a quatre of a milli second.

Sonia: Just barely. Sid is a micro-manager disguised as a team player. you will have to bother a different anxiety ridden slave i am afraid.

Neil: Sid is the type of manager who spends more time polishing speeches than solving problems.

Sonia: hahah accurate

Neil: Speaking of anxiety Tho I have might just need Dia's anxiety pill too as Aerron is gone and you are not willing to help.

Sonia: You can always quit. Anyway, I need to get through this module. He said I need to rewrite half my work from last week.

Neil: Damn. you busy busy.

Sonia: yess, now can we talk later? I have at least 1000 things to figure out till EOD and I'm already more confused than a cat in a laser disco

Neil: you have my goodbyes and my respect.

(Private Teams Chat – Neil <> Vik - 3:34 PM)

Neil: yo, did you get that report from IT on system lag?

also need your help as I have nobody else for today's deadline.

Vik: Yeah. Nothing alarming. CJ just asked my to check system health for literally every system he said and i quote that "virus are communicable so cure every system before we end up in another pandemIc"

Neil: Bruhh, CJ is just a Clown with a LinkedIn Premium Account. His tech illiteracy will one day lead to this team lay off.

Vik: Could be, he already ended 2 relationships when he "accidentally" started the Sam flirting with every living soul rumour.

Neil: don't tell me that's why Adity left!?

Vik: I can neither deny but can surely confirm Sam is a player who Ghosts deadlines and women with equal efficiency.

Can't wait to find out who his next target is!

Neil: damn isn't the player engaged to some techie from Pune? also I think the next target is Sonia, she has mentioned him recently, could be a move.

Vik: Damn I am hating the player and hating the game as well! anyway what can I do for the LORD OF CODE?

Neil: ahh yes, sharing the client's email, let me know if you can help with the firewall issue.

Vik: 'aight

[Private Teams Chat – "LOW-LIVES" - 4:44 PM]
(Members: Neil, Reya, Dia, Maya, Sam, Aerron, Mini, Rishab, Vik, Ritika, Amaan, Sahil, Sonia)

Sam: So… promotions announcement tomorrow. Place your bets, degenerates.

Reya: Degenerates? Coming from you? That's rich.

Sam: I'm rich in confidence.

Ritika: And poor in self-awareness. Anyway, it's obviously between Dia and Sonia.

Maya: Obviously Dia. Experienced, dependable, nice to everyone.

Reya: Sonia. Sharp as hell, defends her work like a gladiator. Plus, half the office has a crush on her.

Sonia: That's not true.

Amaan: It's true.

Mini: It's true.

Sahil: I'm just here so I don't get HR'd.

Neil: Bold of you all to assume Aerron's not in the running.

Aerron: in the running… in the same way a tortoise is in the running with a Ferrari.

Neil: Wow. Hurtful. You led all the deadlines. Worked extra hours. Can't a bro lift another up? Don't sell yourself short man!

Ritika: Yeah, but you also once approved a design file named "final_final_USE_THIS_really_FINAL_v8."

Vik: That's still in the archives. I kept it for evidence.

Dia: Look, if it's Sonia, I'll be happy for her.

Sonia: And if it's Dia, I'll be happy for her.

Maya: See? This is why Dia should get it—mutual respect, actual leadership.

Reya: This is why Sonia should get it—confidence, fresh perspective, doesn't let Sam mansplain font choices.

Sam: Helvetica is superior—

Sonia: I swear, Sam.

Rishab: I say we decide right now via democratic vote.

Neil: Yeah, sure, let's tell management we picked the new leader via the "Low-lives" chat.

Mini: Honestly more reliable than HR.

Amaan: Okay, voting time. Everyone gets one name.

Ritika: My vote's for Dia. Long overdue.

Maya: Dia. Obvious choice

Dia: Sonia. Cos she deserves it!

Sonia: Dia. Nobody more deserving

Reya: Sonia. Youngest manager lessgo baby!

Neil: Aerron. #Menlivesmatter

Sam: Dia. She deserves it more

Aerron: Myself. Can't sell myself short

Vik: Aerron... I'm kidding its Sonia.

Rishab: Dia. She taught me "this PC" is what old people refer to "my computer" icon

Mini: Sonia. Cos she always compliments my makeup!

Sahil: Beauty with brains Sonia.

Amaan: Sonia. My copilot, I trust her with my life.

Ritika: Wait, what's the tally?

Neil: Sonia: 7, Dia: 6...

Aerron: And 1 vote for me, which means I'm the moral winner.

Reya: Sure, champ. Go frame that.

Maya: Wow, close one.

Dia: Congrats, Sonia. Even if it's hypothetical.

Sonia: Thanks... but I'm still betting on Dia.

Neil: Look at that, mutual respect in this chat. Feels weird. Someone insult Sam quick.

Sahil: Sam, your taste in music is tragic.

Sam: Imagine Dragons is -

Everyone: Shut up, Sam.

(Private WhatsApp Chat – Neil <> Reya – 10:41 PM)

Reya: full day without missing me. Someone is feeling dangerous.

Neil: Sorry my love, just got done with the deadline, Vik, Ritika and Sam helped.

Reya: Wow whole squad been putting it in, What did Mr. Flirt Developer do tho? I thought he was done with you guys after yesterday.

Neil: needed someone from front end for a last-minute change and Sonia was busy with Sid's project, he was the second-best option, also he Tried to explain "design flow" to us by quoting Drake lyrics.

Reya: No.

Neil: "Sometimes I go back to the basics, back to the basics."

Reya: I need bleach for my ears.

Neil: Honestly? Iconic. At this point he almost has my respect.

Reya: Everyone knows he's a flirt. Bro has ended more relationships in this office than deadlines at this point.

You could replace the Nurobit logo with his smirk and no one would notice.

Neil: I'm pitching that to marketing. Anyway, I am eating fruits today and that reminded me of you. Remember when I used to bring you finely chopped fresh fruits for my "low Maintenance gf"

Reya: awww yes that was the best, that's how exactly you stole my heart all those years back.

Neil: Who knew my fav berries were Robberies

Reya: hahahah BTW. Did Sonia say anything else about Jay?

Neil: Oh sh*t, yeah. I forgot to tell you earlier. She mentioned he's divorced now.

Reya: WHAT.

Neil: Yeah. Apparently, his wife left him. Some say domestic violence. Just rumours though.

Reya: Ugh. That man gives off "I say I'm emotionally available, but I mean for 6 minutes" energy.

Neil: Accurate. She looked... tense. When she said it.

Reya: Poor girl. She probably has to see his smug face 9–5 now.

Neil: Anyway—enough work talk. How was your day?

Reya: Chaotic. I got a "wellness break" that came with three meetings.

Neil: Very Nurobit of them.

Reya: Also, I found a snack I think you'll like. It's shaped like a cat.

Neil: If I don't get one, this relationship is over.

Reya: Relax. You're my little garbage bin. I save all expired snacks for you.

Neil: I've never felt more seen.

Reya: You're basically home to me, but it's no big deal or anything. Don't worry about it.

Neil: *melts into keyboard*

Reya: Also. When are you flying down? I miss my emotional support coder.

Neil: Soon. When the world stops ending.

Reya: I'll be here. Glowing. Hydrated. Waiting.

(Of course I want to meet Reya. I'd swim across the Arabian Sea if I had to. But in the middle of a pandemic? When the survival odds are basically a coin toss? Yeah, not exactly the romantic weekend getaway I was hoping for.

I need a vacation so badly the mountains have been calling for weeks... and I keep sending them to voicemail. But instead of crisp air and quiet, I'm signing up for Mumbai — a city where "rush hour" is a lifestyle choice.

Last time I visited, the traffic barely moved. My car broke down, I had to push it, and somehow, I still got a speeding ticket. That's not transportation; that's a performance art piece about human suffering.

And let's not forget — Mumbai is hella expensive. Which is great, because I'm traveling at month-end. If a cashier points me toward the "Donate for Poor" jar, I'll probably take some out for myself. Consider it... economic redistribution.

Still, for Reya? I'll risk the pandemic, the traffic, the bankruptcy. She's worth it. Even if I end up spending more time pushing my car than actually holding her hand.)

People Who may Get
Promoted Day Schedule:

Mornings

Logging In and out at Ungodly time
Just to do Bare Minimum work and
laugh at Boss's unfunny jokes

Meetings

Takes Credit for
Team's or Somebody
else's work

Breaks

Hydrate - its important to be
hydrated to countinue being
an Ass Licker

Before Leaving

Snitch on Co workers
to gain leverage and
OfCourse,
Ass - licking

Chapter 04

INFAMOUS LAST WORDS

[Email – From: Sonia <> To: All Employees – 9:00 AM]

Subject: Signing Off, for the last time.

If you're reading this, I'm not here anymore.

It's not one thing. It's everything.
The constant late nights, the endless "urgent" pings, the quiet politics, the whispered half-truths that somehow travel faster than actual work. I've tried to keep my head down, but it's hard when the air around you is full of rumours and side glances.

I've heard the things people think I don't know. I've seen what happens when someone becomes a little *too* good at their job, or when they trust the wrong person. It's funny—everyone claims they want a healthy workplace, but they also keep score in ways that never show up in performance reviews.

Work stress doesn't help. Neither does wondering who will twist your words next. I'm just tired. And I can't take it anymore.

Some of you will read this and feel nothing. Some of you will wonder if I'm talking about you. Either way—live with it.

—Sonia

[Microsoft Teams – #design-strategy – 09:02 AM]

CJ: Team. Please don't panic. We've all received the same email from Sonia. I'm in touch with local authorities. Will share verified information only.

Dev: She was working late with Sid. He might know more.

Sid: She signed off at 9. Said she had a headache.

CJ: Please refrain from speculation. I'll be visiting her apartment shortly with the authorities and will collect company assets. Vik, IT will coordinate with you.

Vik: Understood.

Maya: This can't be real.

Dia: Oh my god. No.

Reya: This doesn't make sense...

Neil: Wasn't she just... busy today? She was FINE.

Jay: I'm shocked. Truly.

I hope this is some mistake.

CJ: Please give the management some time, police are already on their way to Sonia's place.

(I remember feeling nothing at first. Just static. Then my hands started shaking. I reread her message a dozen times, hoping I was wrong. Hoping we all were.)

(Private WhatsApp Chat – Neil <> Reya - 9:00 PM)

Reya: Neil?

Neil: Yeah

Reya: I just got an email from Sonia. Subject line: "Signing off, for the last time"

Neil: Same. I thought it was spam. But it's not.

Reya: I feel sick.

Neil: I talked to her yesterday. She was fine.

Reya: She wasn't. We just didn't know.

Neil: Rey... if she actually...

Reya: Let's not say it until we know.

[Microsoft Teams – #design-strategy – 10:12 AM]

CJ: Hi everyone, I'm deeply saddened to inform you that we've received official confirmation from the police this morning—Sonia Arora passed away last night.

Her family has been informed and are currently on their way. We request everyone to refrain from speculation and respect the family's privacy during this time.

We'll share further updates as appropriate. Resources for mental health support are available on the internal HR page.

Dev: This is unbelievable. Just yesterday she was arguing about button spacing in the UI.

How does someone vanish like that overnight?

Sid: She told me she was exhausted. Said she felt like she couldn't catch a break lately.

I thought she just meant the project.

Mr. Kapoor: This is a tragedy. We will be offering grief counselling. Please reach out to HR for assistance.

Jay: I never got the chance to speak to her properly.

Maya: She was planning something for her parents' anniversary. She said she hadn't been home in years.

Dia: I still can't believe it. I'm so sorry, I just can't.

Neil: I don't know what to say. This doesn't feel real.

Reya: She was just tired, not... this. Not like this.

Sahil: CJ, should we still send the Q4 sprint update? Or...?

Dev: Please give everyone time to process this. We'll regroup later today.

CJ: Yes, we will postpone all standups and sprint updates until further notice. Please take the day to process and check in with yourself or each other.

Rishab: I didn't know her, but I'm taking this really hard. Will skip my intern assignment today for... emotional healing.

Ritika: If anyone needs to vent or cry, I have a Zoom open. Cameras optional. Mics encouraged.

Amaan: Should we like... light a candle on Miro or something?

CJ: Official update: Police confirmed she was found in her apartment late last night. No signs of forced entry. The email was sent from her system. Vik, you'll need to assist with device imaging.

Vik: Already prepped. I'll extract what I can and share with the officers.

CJ: We should do a group Notion doc with Sonia memories. Like a tribute, but make it editable.

(Private WhatsApp Chat – Neil <> Reya – 10:30 AM)

Neil: I still can't believe it. Reading it again doesn't help.

Reya: She wasn't okay. And no one saw it. Or maybe no one wanted to.

Neil: What the hell does she mean by "but it's hard when the air around you is full of rumours and side glances."?

Reya: I think she meant personal stuff.

Or maybe office stuff. Is it really surprising a beautiful single woman who is successful in her career won't be a figure of controversy anywhere she goes?

Neil: successful is a big word, but yes, she was good at her job.

Reya: yup so good that she told me she was up for the same promotion as Dia and Sonia was going to get it.

Neil: Dammit. who got the promotion last year? Dev?

Reya: yup, but this year it was a tough choice between Sonia and her. CJ just told us girlies,.

Neil: woah, I wish Sonia and i should have talked a bit more.

Reya: Don't go there. None of us knew this was coming. But Neil... that email doesn't feel right. It sounds like her, sure. But it's too... polished.

Neil: yeah, but still...

Reya: it's just unfortunate but we can't change anything.

Neil: can't believe, corporate has already suspended her account. it's just some "unknown user" whom I used to talk to a few days back.

Reya: Yeah...I am still staring at the email. Feels unreal.

Neil: "Unreal" is putting it lightly. I keep reading it, thinking I'll spot some hidden clue... but it just sounds like someone tired and done.

Reya: So... you think she actually did it?

Neil: No. Sonia was a lot of things, but she wasn't the type to just... fold. That email doesn't make sense. It's too generic. Too... polished.

Reya: Polished?

Neil: Perfect punctuation. Last time Sonia capitalised anything was "Delhi." And that was only because *"it's the actual capital and no other city deserves that"* — her words, not mine.

Reya: Okay, but maybe if it *was* the last thing she wrote, she might have... you know, paid attention. Made it neat.

Neil: That's the thing — it's neat, but it's not *her*. It's like someone Googled "how to write a suicide note" and hit send. Sonia wouldn't leave without making her point, loud and clear.

Reya: Yeah... you're right. She'd have at least thrown in one personal jab, just to haunt the person forever.

Neil: Exactly. This email has no teeth. And Sonia never went quietly.

Reya: She *is* strong-headed. But... I can't ignore what I know either.

Neil: Go on.

Reya: She's had anxiety attacks before. Not a secret between us girls.

We have this little "girlies" chat—me, Sonia, Dia, Maya, and Ritika. Kind of our safe zone to talk about work crap, bad dates, life.

Neil: And?

Reya: A while back, Sonia opened up about getting panic attacks.

Dia even jumped in with her usual know-it-all tone and told her about these anti-anxiety meds.

She actually... "prescribed" them, in her own way.

Neil: Wait—Dia isn't a doctor.

Reya: Nope. But she has a pharmacist cousin and enough medical trivia to bluff her way through WebMD.

She used to check in on Sonia regularly: "Are you taking them? Don't skip." To be fair Dia would regularly ask us as well, I think Maya also took prescription from a doctor and got meds but I don't think she is also taking them.

Neil: And was Sonia taking them?

Reya: Not anymore. Past couple of weeks, she's been saying she's feeling fine. Happier. Calmer. Even joked she didn't need the meds anymore.

Neil: Any reason why?

Reya: I think... new boyfriend.

Neil: Boyfriend? She never told me.

Reya: She didn't tell most people. But she hinted in the group chat—inside jokes, little smiley emojis out of nowhere. It wasn't hard to put two and two together.

Neil: So you think... she got happy because of him, stopped the meds, and then... what?

Reya: And then maybe he tried to end it. Maybe it was too sudden. She's been... intense about relationships before.

Neil: That's a hell of a leap though. New relationship, early stage—why would she spiral so hard over that?

Reya: Exactly. It *doesn't* fully make sense. Like I said, Sonia was strong-headed. If a guy messed her around, she'd usually scorch-earth the man's reputation before ever blaming herself.

Neil: So why now?

Reya: That's the thing. I don't know. Part of me thinks the timing is too neat. Happy one week, "signing off, for the last time" email the next. And remember—no one outside our girlies group even knew about her meds.

Neil: Which means if anyone *did* want to make it look like suicide...

Reya: ...they could use that as leverage. The whole "she had anxiety, she was unstable" angle.

Neil: That's unsettling.

Reya: Welcome to my brain right now. I can't stop replaying our last conversation—she was laughing. Like, actually laughing.

Neil: So, officially, we have three possibilities:

1. She really did it, sudden emotional trigger.
2. Something else entirely happened, and someone's framing it as suicide.
3. This is the worst office wellness campaign ever.

Reya: That last one is not funny.

Neil: I wasn't joking. HR could pull something like that.

Reya: ...sadly, true.

Neil: Okay. For now, keep this meds detail between us. No point throwing it in the open until we know more.

Reya: Agreed. And Neil?

Neil: Yeah?

Reya: If I find out who the boyfriend is, you'll be the first to know. I still think he is the killer.

Neil: I'll hold you to that.

(That morning, everything changed. She wasn't just gone. She left behind a grenade. One that hadn't exploded yet.)

[Forwarded Email by CJ – Mumbai Police Preliminary Crime Scene Report]

Subject: Sonia Arora – Case No. MUM/230925

Date of Incident: 24th September

Time of Estimated Death: Between 11:45 PM and 12:15 AM IST

Location: Flat 4B, Sunridge Towers, Andheri West, Mumbai

Victim: Sonia Arora, Female, Age 26

Occupation: UX Designer at Nurobit Solutions Pvt Ltd

Residence: Sunridge Towers, Andheri West

Preliminary Findings:

- **Cause of Death (Presumed):** Ingestion of a toxic compound consistent with the presence of high levels of Alprazolam, delivered through a consumable liquid—suspected to be coffee.
- **Position Found:** Victim was discovered on her living room couch, fully clothed, with a laptop bag on the adjacent table and one takeaway coffee cup present.
- **Time of Death Estimation:** Based on gastric contents, body temperature, and last digital activity (laptop shutdown at 10:57 PM), time of death is narrowed to a 30-minute window between 11:45–12:15 PM.

Crime Scene Observations:

- **Forced Entry:** No visible signs of forced entry.
- **Access Points:** Main door was locked from the inside using the latch. Bedroom windows were found slightly open.

- **Surveillance Footage:** No surveillance footage found due to lack of cameras around victims home, last seen leaving office premises at 6:40.
- **Interior:** No signs of struggle or disarray. Toxicology confirmed coffee in the cups had elevated chemical levels. Toxicology results indicate the presence of high levels of Alprazolam, a benzodiazepine primarily prescribed for acute anxiety disorders. The concentration found in the victim's bloodstream significantly exceeded the therapeutic dosage and falls within the known fatal range.
- **Smartcard Discovery:** A smartcard issued to one "Dev Singh" was found inserted in the laptop's USB port. Device had been chemically cleaned, likely to erase fingerprints.
- **Call Details:** on the day of the victims' death she called her mother in the morning and two calls to Siddharth Bhattacharya that didn't connect.

Status:

- **Pending:** Interrogation of suspects Siddharth Bhattacharya and Dev Singh (scheduled).
- **Forensics:** Awaiting lab confirmation on poison origin and digital recovery from hard drive.
- **Classification:** *Suspicious Death – Under Investigation*

PRELIMINARY CONCLUSION:

Likely suicide by overdose. However, absence of handwriting suicide notes verification, questionable smartcard activity, and timeline inconsistencies have not ruled out the possibility of foul play. Further digital forensics and mail verification pending.

Filed by:

Inspector S. More

Mumbai Homicide Division

DCP Zone 9 (Under Supervision)

[Microsoft Teams – Dev:lopers (Dev, Aerron, Neil)– 01:02 AM]

Aerron: BROO

Neil: Bro. Your smart card was found in Sonia's *laptop*. In her *house*. What the actual—

Aerron: Man, I saw it in the police report and legit choked on my protein shake.

Neil: It was found *in Sonia's laptop*, Dev. *Inside* the goddamn machine. Like it moved in, paid rent, and called it home.

Dev: I KNOW.

Dev: Just got back from giving my statement. police were polite. Polite in that "we-think-you-did-it" kind of way.

Neil: What'd you tell them?

Dev: The damn truth. I lost the card. Two days *before*. Emailed CJ, Vik issued me a new one the same evening.

The timeline checks out. I've only been logging in with the replacement since.

Aerron: So... someone picked up your old card and just shoved it in her laptop?

Dev: I guess?? I didn't even know it was missing until I needed it for access and realized it was gone.

Neil: You think she could've had it? By mistake?

Dev: No clue. I wasn't working directly with her last week.

Hell, I barely spoke to her after the product pitch.

Aerron: Either someone planted it, or that card's got a mind of its own. Like the Sorting Hat but for HR violations.

Neil: Damn, man. They think you're involved?

Dev: They didn't say it. But when something with your name on it is found in a crime scene its very much "please come sit in the interrogation chair and ruin your week."

Aerron: Bro. That's dark. And they made you go *after hours*?

Dev: Yep. Right after work. No lawyer, no snacks. I should've brought CJ at least.

Neil: That's the one time his corporate empathy script would've been useful.

Dev: I'm telling you—someone's framing me. I don't know why, or who, but I've got a goddamn target on my back.

Aerron: For what it's worth, we got you, bro. But this surely is a task of a women! Only they can pull this sneaky shit off!

Neil: Yeah. We'll figure this out. Just don't pull a Gone Girl on us.

Dev: Don't worry. If I was going to fake anything, it'd be my attendance.

[Private WhatsApp Chat – Neil <> Reya - 10:43 PM]

Neil: Dev's smart card?

Reya: I always had a bad feeling about him being too nonchalant.

Neil: being nonchalant isn't a crime. also, we talked to him and so did the police.!

Reya: well obviously, his smart card in the dead girl's laptop is basically writings on the wall. Also making someone drink coffee with Alprazolam is!

Neil: what even is that?

Reya: I googled, its key ingredient of anxiety pills. Which i know she had as Dia convinced Maya and Sonia after a 2 hr TED TALK on perks of pills.

Neil: damn, do you also take them?

Reya: nope? didn't feel like taking one, though some days I come to close, but then i see talk to you.

Neil: aww.

Reya: So, it's possible she took them with coffee, I mean she had the tools its possible but Dev's smart card in her laptop is the question I have in mind.

Neil: I figured that the suicide email is not written by Sonia as she never used perfect punctuations or capitalise first letters. and time of death confirms that mail was sent hrs after she died.

Reya: Could be scheduled email. but what about the laptop wiped clean.

Neil: clearly someone who typed the mail wiped the laptop.

Reya: Do you think it was...

Neil: I think someone else wrote that email.

Reya: Then we're looking at murder.

Neil: Yeah.

Chapter 05

THE UNUSUAL SUSPECTS

[Email – From: CJ <> To: All Employees – 9:03 AM]

Subject: Request for Internal Review Submissions – Sonia A

Team,

As part of protocol, we're compiling an internal timeline of interactions with Sonia. Please send in your statements by EOD today, even if you have nothing significant to add. This is a difficult time for all of us, and your cooperation is appreciated.

Regards,

CJ

HR – Strategy & Design dept.

Nurobit Solutions

[Email – From: Neil <> To: CJ – 10:20 AM]

Subject: Re: Internal Review – Sonia

Hey CJ,

I last spoke to Sonia on the 23rd during project updates. She was quiet, but nothing out of the ordinary. She didn't seem low or distracted, just buried in work. I honestly didn't sense anything unusual.

We cracked a few jokes, but that was it. We always joked about killing ourselves before doing another client's revision or excel being the death of us but i never felt she took suicide as an option. I still don't believe that. Let me know if you need anything else.

-Neil V. Mehta

Automation Consultant – Strategy & Design dept.

Nurobit Solutions

[Email – From: Dev <> To: CJ – 10:33 AM]

Subject: Internal Review – Sonia

Hi CJ,

Sonia was one of the sharpest minds I've worked with — fast, focused, and always one step ahead. She had a way of asking the one question everyone else missed.

Sure, she was intense. But in a place where people still forget to rename files, that intensity mattered.

We didn't always agree, but I respected her more than I ever admitted.

Whatever people are saying now — it doesn't change the fact that she was damn good. And she didn't deserve this.

Happy to cooperate if you need more.

– Dev Singh

Associate – Strategy & Design dept.

Nurobit Solutions

[Email – From: Ritika <> To: CJ – 10:59 PM]

To: CJ

Subject: RE: Review Submission

Hey,

Don't really have much to say. She once complimented my screen wallpaper. That's all I remember.

Hope that helps.

– Ritika Kesarvani

Sr. Developer – Strategy & Design dept.

Nurobit Solutions

[Email – From: Sid <> To: CJ – 10:59 PM]

Hi CJ,

Sonia was reporting to me on the front-end optimization project these past few weeks. We didn't always agree, but I respected how committed she was to getting things right.

On the night in question, I dropped by her apartment briefly to hand over my smartcard. She needed access to some classified project folders and her credentials weren't enough. I left soon after. It wasn't more than a five-minute stop.

I didn't notice anything off that evening. She seemed tired, sure, but not... unwell. We'd both been pushing long hours. I didn't imagine things could spiral like this.

I hope the investigation brings some clarity. She deserved that much.

– Siddharth Bhattacharya

Associate – Strategy & Design dept.

Nurobit Solutions

[Email – From: Reya <> To: CJ – 11:02 AM]

Subject: Re: Internal Review

Hi,

Sonia and I didn't work closely, but we chatted occasionally. Last week, she mentioned she was excited to attend her parents' 25th anniversary next month. I remember because she was hunting for a gift and complaining that her dad didn't need another watch.

She was making plans. This whole thing... doesn't make sense.

- Reya Sharma

Sr. Graphic Designer – Strategy & Design dept.

Nurobit Solutions

[Email – From: Shyam (Office Guard) <> To: CJ – 12:00 PM]

Subject: Re: Sonia madam

Sir,

I saw Sonia madam leave building Tuesday night. She looked tired but not upset. She said "Goodnight bhaiya" like always. I see her often, and she always say bye. I did not see anyone else with her. Only Sonia madam.

Thank you,

Shyam Mathur

Security Guard

Nurobit Solutions

[Email – From: *Shankar (Canteen Supervisor)* **<> To: CJ – 1:36 PM]**

To: CJ

Subject: Confidential Notes on the Matter

Respected sir,

I am deeply sad about Sonia madam. She used to ask for *extra chutney* without shame and that shows her kind nature. She never wasted food and always returned her coffee cup.

Regarding possible suspects:

- I have seen Sid sir many times standing weirdly near her desk.

- Also, Jay sir always orders cold coffee even when weather is cold. Suspicious man.
- Dev sir came twice last week, looked very stressed. I think guilt.
- Maya madam always silent. She once ate only one Idli. Not normal.
- That intern Rishab.. so happy. Maybe hiding something?

I watch *Crime Patrol* daily and can help in further investigation.

Regards,

Shankar Devgun

Canteen Operations: ground floor

Nurobit Solutions

[Email – From: Dia<> To: CJ – 2:05 PM]

Subject: Re: Internal Review - Sonia

Hi CJ,

I wasn't in close contact with Sonia in the past few days. We were on separate deliverables. Last I recall, she seemed tired. But Sonia always pushed through. I don’t know what to say. I knew about her anxiety attacks but didn't know it was this bad.

Regards,

Dia Dutta

Sr. Data Analyst – Strategy & Design dept.

Nurobit Solutions

[Email – From: Sahil <> To: CJ – 2:09 PM]

Subject: Internal Review

Hi,

I didn't interact with Sonia much apart from a "hi" or "good morning." But she always wore perfume that reminded me of that Sonia store scent. The irony isn't lost on me.

Sorry. That probably wasn't appropriate.

Anyway, I don't know anything else.

Thanks,

Sahil Rajput

Back end developer – Strategy & Design dept.

Nurobit Solutions

[Email – From: Maya <> To: CJ – 2:29 PM]

Subject: Re: Internal Review - Sonia

Hi,

Sonia was... efficient. Quiet. I didn't know her personally, but she was good at what she did.

We all have rough days, and maybe she had more than her share. But she didn't deserve this.

Thanks,

Maya Kapoor

Jr. Data Analyst – Strategy & Design dept.

Nurobit Solutions

[Email – From: Amaan <> To: CJ – 2:56 PM]

Hey CJ,

I've been staring at this email for over an hour now, trying to find the right words. But how do you summarize someone like Sonia in a few lines? How do you explain a comet to a spreadsheet?

Sonia wasn't just a colleague. She was a vibe. A mood. A carefully curated aesthetic. The kind of person who could shut down a bad idea with just a glance and then comfort you with a meme five minutes later. Working with her was like learning from a strict professor who moonlighted as your slightly chaotic best friend. Her Figma skills were divine, her sarcasm sharper than our team's best UI, and honestly... yeah, I had a bit of a crush on her. Who didn't?

There was this one time I asked her for help on a presentation, and she said, "Amaan, this looks like you designed it on MS Paint during an earthquake." I never felt more seen. Or roasted.

She was kind, but never fake. Helpful, but never a pushover. Her messages were always efficient, peppered with emojis only when deserved. I once saved a Slack message she sent me because I thought it was the nicest anyone had ever been to me professionally.

This whole thing doesn't sit right. She didn't seem like someone who would give up. She was talking about going home for Diwali. She was excited about a new feature rollout. She even yelled at me for using Comic Sans in a design brief two days ago.

I don't know what happened. But I know we lost someone who actually mattered. To the team. To the office. To me.

I'll miss her. Every day.

– Amaan malik

Jr. Graphic Designer – Strategy & Design dept.

Nurobit Solutions

[Email – From: Sam <> To: CJ – 3:15 PM]

Subject: Re: Internal Review - Sonia

Hey,

I collaborated with Sonia once on a sprint last month. We barely spoke, to be honest. Just task comments and the occasional clarification.

Can't say much else.

Regards,

-Samarth Pathak

Sr. Front end developer – Strategy & Design dept.

Nurobit Solutions

[Email – From: Mini <> To: CJ – 3:37 PM]

Subject: Re: Internal Review

Hi CJ,

Sonia and I didn't talk much. Just smiles in the hallway and once she complimented my makeup.

She seemed really focused. I wish I had more to say.

-Mini Kapoor

Brand Evangelist – Strategy & Design dept.

Nurobit Solutions

[Internal Teams Chat – #IT-Support – 5:47 PM]

Neil: Dude was Dev's access card missing from few days? just needed to confirm.

Vik: yup. your boi gave him the replacement himself. you don't think he did it right?

Neil: ofc not, but Reya thinks he is hiding something because he doesn't speak much.

Vik: in my life i never questioned a woman's guts but this seems far fetched.

Neil: although its definitely not Dev, I will find out who murdered Sonia and framed Dev

Vik: alright Sherlock, let me know if you and Watson run into some tech issue and keep me posted when you find the killer.

Neil: sure, will raise a ticket when we find the murderer

[Private WhatsApp – Neil <> Reya – 6:02 PM]

Reya: So... I've been thinking.

Neil: Uh-oh.

Reya: No, seriously. Its Jay right.

Neil: Jay?? Mr. I-got-a-Master's-in-manipulation-from-London?

Reya: EXACTLY. Like, we *know* he has a violent streak. Sonia told you he was possessive. And now—she's gone.

Neil: That's not evidence, babe. That's an episode of *Indian Crime Patrol*.

Reya: Okay but listen—he has motive, history, AND a fragile ego wrapped in Sonia perfume. That's textbook.

Neil: Also textbook? Me failing every test before noon. Doesn't make me a criminal.

Reya: 😁 Don't dodge this. What if he found out she was dating someone else? Lost it. Boom. Rage blackout.

Neil: I mean... I *have* seen him rehearse his smiles in the Zoom camera. So that tracks.

Reya: I'm telling you. Men who drink protein shakes without blinking scare me.

Neil: So... me?

Reya: Nooo you blink like five times a second when you're thinking. It's cute. Like a stressed-out hamster.

Neil: Thank you? I think? you think very highly of me.

Reya: Back to Jay—he even *talks* like a motivational quote trying too hard. "Happy to be here." "Excited to contribute." *Who says that* unironically?

Neil: A man with *something to hide*.

Reya: Exactly! And no one even looked into him seriously. Just because he smiles and wears loafers with no socks.

Neil: That *is* suspicious behaviour, not gonna lie. Loafers without socks is basically: "I've buried secrets... and maybe bodies."

Reya: See? Sonia *knew* how to spot red flags. That's why she dumped him. But maybe he couldn't handle it.

Neil: Hmm. Then why kill her now? Months later?

Reya: Obsessive types don't work on your normal breakup timeline. They simmer. Like emotional biryani.

Neil: Okay that was beautiful. I want that on a mug.

Reya: "Emotional biryani" could be my Instagram bio

Neil: I'll unfollow.

Reya: So, do you think it could be him?

Neil: I don't know. Maybe. But honestly? Something about this feel... off. Too obvious. But we should start with him.

Reya: cool, i'll meet him in the office tomorrow, will have a lil one to one. Any questions you want me to ask other than his past relationships?

Neil: Yeah, his moisturiser brand name and why did he kill Sonia?

Reya: straight to the point, my type of man

Neil: I thought men who don't moisturise is a red flag

Reya: Don't worry. You're my favourite walking red flag.

Neil: That's because I wear it like a cape.

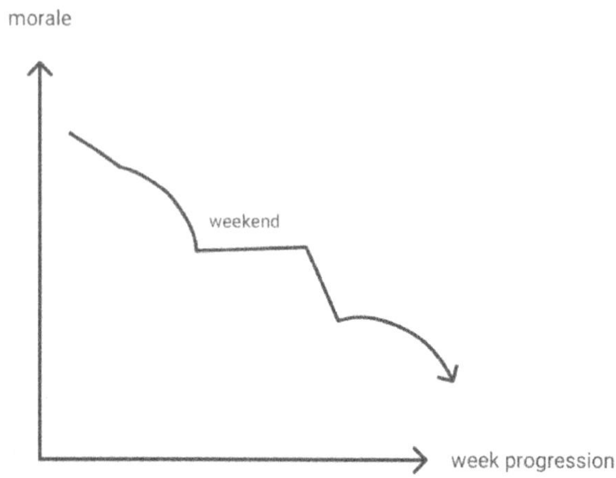

Company Morale Decreases After mandatory grief workshop

CHAPTER 06

FOR YOUR FYI ONLY

[Microsoft Teams – #design-strategy – 09:49 AM]

CJ: Good morning, team. Please submit your Q3 Manager Feedback Forms by EOD.

Yes, even if your manager "already knows you're amazing." Corporate needs it.

Mini: Submitted mine at 9 AM ▯

Dia: Do we *really* have to fill that self-assessment part again?

CJ: It's called self-reflection, Dia. That's how we grow.

Maya: Some of us would rather self-destruct, thanks.

Reya: Mine's just "lost a colleague last week, still finished deadlines." Is that enough?

CJ: Gold star for emotional restraint.

Neil: I wrote "still not fired" and hit submit.

CJ: You know what, I'll allow it.

Sid: Let's try to focus, team. We're still short-staffed. Maya, Dia — I've looped you both into the Sharma Designs handover file. Please check and update status.

Dev: Neil, Aerron — help me wrap the Pine AI edge case audit today?

Aerron: Sure. I have opinions about it. Uninformed ones. But opinions. If i review it, you might as well consider it done.

Neil: Can confirm. Man, once reviewed a script without reading it.

Aerron: it's called muscle mind machine connection.

Dev: Children, focus.

Sam: Good morning all. Let me know if anyone needs help with the quarter-end backlog.

Sahil: You volunteering for extra work?

Sam: Can't a guy just be helpful?

Sahil: last time you volunteered for extra work you were are useful as screen door on a submarine.

Sam: never mind I'm taking 2nd half off.

Rishab: same.

[Private Teams Chat – Neil <> Vik – 11:39 AM]

Neil: You saw Sam's messages this morning?

Vik: You mean his "just tell me if anyone needs help" PR campaign?

Neil: Exactly. Has he always been this eager?

Vik: No, but Sonia dying *did* mess everyone up. Some overcompensate.

Neil: You think he's overcompensating?

Vik: Or panicking.

Neil: Interesting. Nowadays, every time he speaks its like watching a watching a snowman take a tan in the sun.

Vik: yeahh. Want me to run anything?

Neil: did you find something related to Sonia on his system? my detective sense is tingling.

Vik: yes, but nothing concrete. same generic good morning to the most beautiful model in Nurobit to like half a dozen of different colleagues.

Neil: Something tells me he is guilty.

Vik: Well, he looked like that way before someone died in this office.

Neil: I think i'll talk to him and see what sup.

Vik: try rejecting the coffee if he offers one.

Neil: haha I'm lactose intolerant from now on.

[Private Teams Chat – Neil <> Sam – 1:12 PM]

Neil: Hey man. You free?

Sam: Yeah, what's up?

Neil: Just... wanted to check in. You okay?

Sam: Yeah. Just weirded out, like everyone.

Neil: I get that. I was going through some of the UI handover Sonia did before everything... went down. You two worked closely, right?

Sam: Yeah. On and off. She was... sharp. Quiet when she was stressed.

Neil: Did she ever mention anyone? Like, being in trouble? Or... afraid?

Sam: Okay, I don't know if I should say this. But it's been eating me up.

Neil: Go on.

Sam: Sonia and I... we weren't close-close, but we... hooked up. Once.

Neil: When?

Sam: Like, two weeks back. It was late, we were working on that client handover deck. One thing led to another. But it wasn't... emotional. I didn't lead her on or anything.

Neil: And after?

Sam: She acted like it never happened. Just back to business. I respected that. I swear.

Neil: Why didn't you say anything earlier?

Sam: Because I didn't want it to look like I used her. And now, with her gone... it just feels wrong to pretend it didn't happen.

Neil: Did anyone else know?

Sam: Maybe Sid? He saw us leave together that night. But he never said anything.

[Private WhatsApp Chat – Neil <> Reya – 3:27 PM]

Neil: So... Sam just confessed something.

Reya: Oof. Did he kill someone?

Neil: No. But apparently, he and Sonia... were involved. Once.

Reya: Wait WHAT.

Neil: "One-time thing," he said. After a late-night work sprint.

Reya: And we thought *Dev* was the dark horse...

Neil: Still could be. But this does muddy the timeline. If they weren't *together*, but hooked up once... motive? Jealousy?

Reya: Or maybe guilt. Maybe it meant more to *him*.

Neil: He said it didn't. Or that she didn't want more.

Reya: That doesn't mean he didn't want more. People lie to save face, especially men with engagement rings.

Neil: True. Reya... you remember when Sonia said Sam was acting weird?

Reya: Yeah. Long stares. Flirty texts.

Neil: What if she tried to keep things professional after that one night, and he couldn't?

Reya: That... would be motive. Not enough to point fingers, but something to file away.

[Private Teams Chat – Neil <> Aerron – 5:32 PM]

Aerron: What's with you today? You've been on edge.

Neil: Found out Sam and Sonia... had a thing.

Aerron: Ew. For real?

Neil: Yep. Post-midnight code sprint turned candlelight.

Aerron: I thought he was engaged. Crazy.

Neil: I just don't know what to think anymore. Everyone's got layers.

Aerron: You're the only onion I trust, buddy.

Neil: Touching.

Aerron: He really hooked up with Sonia? What happened to her standards?

Neil: He said, and I quote, "It just happened. We were both lonely."

Aerron: Bro. That's not loneliness. That's HR violation with a scented candle.

Neil: Post-office "wine and unwind" turned into "whine and unzipped." Sam probably slid in like a discount therapist with muscles.

Aerron: Honestly, I thought Jay would be the one with skeletons. But now Sam's confession feels like when the waiter admits he touched your food, but only *after* you ate it.

Neil: SAME. His face just screams, "I've watched *You* on Netflix and took notes.

Aerron: And that voice. British but bankrupt.

Neil: LMAOOO. He just looks like the kind of guy who says "I was raised right" and then parks in wheelchair zones.

Aerron: Wait wait—before we get carried away—did you push the latest fix for MobiNet? The "add to cart" function is crashing on Safari. Client's freaking out.

Neil: Yeah, pushed it this morning. Safari bug's on their side. I left notes in the shared doc with diagrams. Clients love rectangles.

Aerron: God-tier advice.

Neil: Corporate gaslighting. We're so back.

Aerron: Honestly though...Sonia deserved better. Literally anyone but Sam

Neil: Sam gives the energy of "I listen to women" but calls all his exes crazy.

Aerron: You think Sonia regretted it?

Neil: I think she was tired. Sam was... there.

Aerron: *"There"*—the lowest bar in male contribution.

Neil: That bar is underground.

Aerron: She deserved so much better, man.

Neil: agreed, she may be dead but still has more presence than 90% of the team.

Aerron: Agreed, so nay plans for the weekend?

Neil: was thinking of solving this murder or just finish that marvel movie with the thing in the sky and the guy from space threatens the universe. You? Didn't you have a date?

Aerron: No bro, all the women I have been DM'ing are following this trend of deleting their DP and changing their username to "Instagramer" apparently. I'm waiting for at least one of them to reply.

Neil: Something tells me its going to be a looong wait.

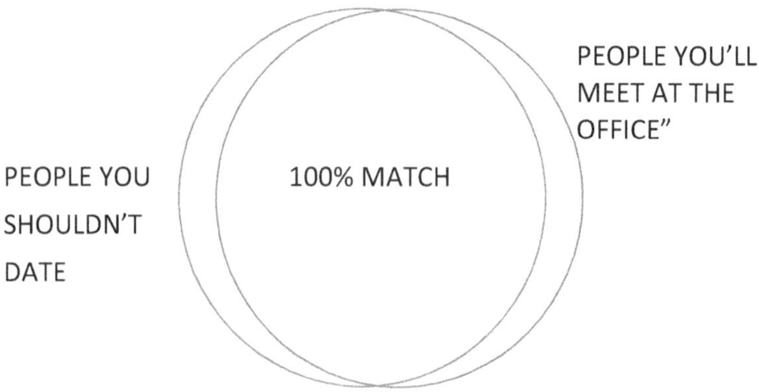

CHAPTER 07

HIRING FOR THE POSITION OF "MURDERER"

[Microsoft Teams – #design-strategy – 09:38 AM]

CJ: Morning, team. And for those who weren't able to yesterday, Please remember to submit your Q3 Manager Feedback Forms by EOD

Mini: Good morning!

Vik: I wrote "I am trying my best in this economy."

Sahil: Mine says "survived another quarter without quitting."

CJ: I swear I read every one of these.

Dia: Submitted.

Sam: Good morning, all. Let's keep it tight today 💪

Maya: Morning. Sent mine too.

Jay: Done. Good morning team.

Dev: Hey all. Neil, Aerron—need you both on client sync at 11. Sid, can you review Maya's draft on the CX flows?

Sid: Yep, on it.

Aerron: On it. Also, Maya—love the new Figma labels. Super clean.

Maya: Thanks, Aerron :)

Neil: on it.

[Email – From: CJ <> To: All Employees – 12:42 PM]

Subject: Weekly Mental Wellness Resource – "Dealing with Loss in the Workplace"

Hi everyone,

Please find attached this week's mental health bulletin. I know we're all processing things differently, and Nurobit is committed to supporting you. Reach out to HR if you'd like to speak to a counsellor.

Take care,

CJ

(The day stretched long. Emails stayed unread. Everyone had an opinion, but no one had clarity. And somewhere between silence and suspicion, Sam typed and erased a message seventeen times.)

[Private Teams Chat – "LOW-LIVES" - 11:44 AM]
(Members: Neil, Reya, Dia, Maya, Sam, Aerron, Mini, Rishab, Vik, Ritika, Amaan, Sahil, offline member)

Vik: adding Jay to the group

Sahil: What is this? Why am I here?

Ritika: Same. I thought this was for about the promotions.

Amaan: I thought someone died again.

Neil: Well.

Aerron: Technically...

Mini: Wait. Is this about Sonia?

Vik: Yes. It's important. No time to explain nicely.

Straight question.

Does anyone think Jay could've been involved in Sonia's death?

Jay: WHAT THE F—

Vik: Guys please don't add anyone else. this is just to answer did jay ctrl + alt + delete her?

Sam: ngl... he *did* show up day after her death looking like a washed-up Bond villain.

Maya: I agree its sus, I have the same question.

Ritika: yes same.

Neil: Be honest Jay.

Neil: Where *were* you that night?

Jay: Oh my god.

Jay: I wasn't even near Sonia's apartment.

Jay: I was at Mini's place.

Sahil: 😳

Mini: Sorry??

Amaan: Broooooooo

Ritika: SCANDAL!

Aerron: Wait. Are we talking *Mini*Mini?

Jay: Yes. The CEO's daughter Mini.

Jay: I went there to talk about a personal loan. She wasn't answering my messages. I showed up uninvited.

Neil: So... you just materialized at her house?

Jay: I was desperate.

Jay: I didn't even go in. I rang the bell. She let me crash on the porch couch. That's it.

Mini: He's not lying.

Mini: I have CCTV footage.

Mini: Timestamped. Shows both of us on my porch arguing. Then him sleeping like a dead man.

Sam: Wrong phrase bro 😬

Mini: Poor choice of words. But yes. He didn't move all night.

Vik: phew, well now we have 0 leads.

Mini: Wait wait. Why were y'all arguing?? 👀

Mini: That's not relevant.

Maya: That means it's *very* relevant.

Ritika: I'm making popcorn.

Aerron: So we just accused a man of murder and now we're discussing porch sleepovers.

Neil: Peak Monday.

Jay: You all owe me an apology.

Sahil: I mean. yeah man sorryy

Amaan: So... he's innocent?

Vik: For now.

Jay: That's not comforting.

Mini: Don't worry. I've got your back.

Jay: Thanks... I guess.

Sam: Wait can we leave this group now?

Neil: Only after we rename it to something iconic.

Aerron: "Jay Did It But He Didn't"

Reya: "Porch Crimes & Alibis"

Ritika: "CCTV and Chill"

Sahil: I vote "Loan Me an Alibi"

Vik: Winner.

Jay: Since we're playing *Among Us* in real life, I have a question.

Where were the *rest* of you the night Sonia died?

Neil: Bangalore. With my laptop. And my guilt.

Amaan: Kolkata. I live with my mother. If I even tried murder, she'd whack me with a belan.

Sahil: Jaipur. Remote life, baby. Closest thing I've killed is productivity.

Ritika: Lucknow. Watching *Shark Tank India* and judging people with bad pitch decks.

Vik: Wow. All the WFH gang got strong alibis stronger than their Wi-fi.

Jay: What about the *Mumbai crew*?

Dia: Me and Maya went out for drinks. Post-office bar hop. Bombay brewery. do you also want to know what we ordered?

We were there till midnight.

Maya: Yeah. I have a photo from that night. Blurry but timestamped. Also I drank half a Virgin Mojito and had an existential crisis in the washroom, so I'm sure the staff remembers me.

Fine. Rishab? What about you?

Rishab: Uh. I dunno. I think I was home? Maybe scrolling memes. I black out around 9 PM emotionally. You know how it is.

Neil: So you have no alibi.

Rishab: Exactly. I'm murder-adjacent only by accident.

Sam: Wait is it just me or is this turning into *Clue: Corporate Edition*?

Reya: Except the killer's probably still in the chat.

Jay: Okay. Reya? What were *you* doing the night Sonia died? Can't just sit there and drop poetic one-liners.

Reya: Excuse you. I was on a video call. With Neil. From 9 PM to 2 AM. He watched me spiral about client feedback and then we fell asleep mid-FaceTime.

Neil: Confirmed. She monologued about fonts for 30 minutes. No one fakes that level of Helvetica-based pain.

Amaan: That's cute. Slightly traumatic. But cute.

Jay: Alright. That's solid. Aerron?

Aerron: Okay don't laugh. I was sick. Had a throat infection and mild fever. Got a doctor's note. Also watched *Harry Potter and the Half-Blood Prince* to feel better.

Ritika: Wait. *Half-Blood Prince*??

Sahil: Ew. The worst one. You *are* the killer.

Maya: People who voluntarily watch that movie are capable of anything.

Vik: he killed vibes for sure.

Aerron: EXCUSE ME?? I was emotional and congested. And this part has the best cinematography and I like Slughorn!

Neil: That's even worse bro.

Mini: Honestly, lock him up in the Azkaban. Just for taste.

Neil : Okay but jokes aside—We've ruled out me, Reya, Neil, Amaan, Sahil, Ritika, Mini, Maya, Dia, Aerron, Rishab (somehow)... And the Police already checked Dev's alibi. CCTV, witness, the whole shebang. So...

Vik: Only one name left.

Amaan: Sid.

Sam: Oh sh*t..

Aerron: So are we saying it's Sid?

Neil: Let's just say... it's not looking good for him.

Maya: I mean. We all knew the man was shady. We just didn't think *murder-y*.

Jay: Now I feel better about getting blamed earlier. Thanks guys.

Sahil: Happy to wrongly accuse, anytime.

People who can be murderer purely based on "Vibes"

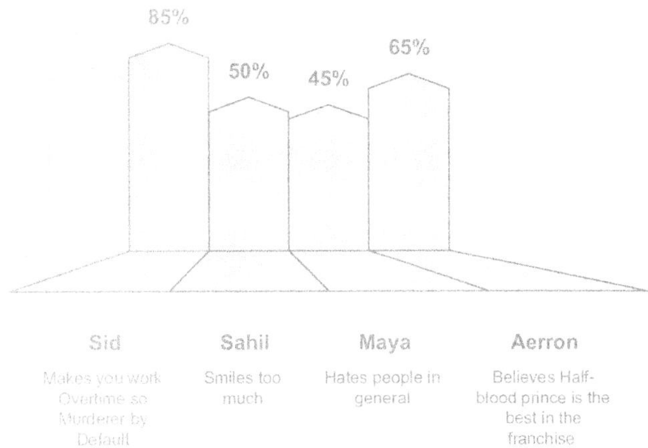

CHAPTER 08

THE DEVIL WEARS TIMEPIECES

[Microsoft Teams – #design-strategy – 09:16 AM]

CJ: Morning team. Let's stay focused today — I know emotions are high, but deadlines remain. Please submit your revised project timelines by EOD.

Vik: Not sure which is harder — the debugging or the grieving. 😵‍💫🌌

Sid: Will need an extra day for our module. Sonia had half the updates; I'll cover the rest.

Dev: Understood. Coordinate with Dia and keep me looped in.

Neil: If you need help Sid then i am available today.

Dev: you are?

Neil: yes, I'm almost done and Aerron is taking care of the rest.

Aerron: Yes

Dia: Neil can you please cover our work as well? i have lost my will to work.

Maya: You're not alone.

Reya: We've got each other. Let's just take it one hour at a time.

[Private Teams Chat – Neil <> Vik – 9:12 PM]

Neil: Yo, Vik. You got those login traces from the night Sonia... you know?

Vik: My dude I have something for you. And before you ask, no, I didn't "hack" anything. This is literally my job.

Neil: You say that like HR hasn't sent you at least two "please stop scaring people with your powers" emails.

Vik: Three. One of them had "We are concerned for morale" in bold. I printed it out.

Neil: For... inspiration?

Vik: For my fridge. It's my version of employee of the month.

Neil: Okay, fridge trophies aside, what did you find?

Vik: Sid's logs are... let's say, not boring.

Neil: Define "not boring."

Vik: He didn't log in from home Wi-Fi. At 9:27 PM, he connected using a hotspot named... "Sid's iPhone."

Neil: Wow, real incognito stuff. CIA should hire him.

Vik: Yeah, the man hides secrets like a toddler hides candy—visible from space.

Neil: And where was this hotspot?

Vik: Mumbai. Facing the beach. GPS pings from a location that screams "either date night or body drop-off point."

Neil: Please tell me it was a Starbucks by the shore.

Vik: Nope. No coffee shops nearby. Closest place is a "Sea Breeze Couples Retreat" motel and few spas.

Neil: Oh my god.

Vik: Which, for the record, has *terrible* password security. Not that I checked.

Neil: Vik.

Vik: What? I was curious.

Neil: Why would Sid need a hotspot there?

Vik: Either to avoid home IP logs... or he was streaming "Bridgerton" for ambiance.

Neil: This is solid. You're a genius.

Vik: Obviously.

Neil: What do you even do on weekends?

Vik: Laundry, stream Cricket, save the city from criminals dressed as clowns, and hit gym as well.

Neil: ...ok middle class batman?

Vik: parents are alive so not there yet.

Neil: Its not who you are underneath but what you do that defines you!

Vik: yeah but its just... insomnia with extra steps.

Neil: No dates? Girlfriend? Boyfriend?

Vik: Single by choice.

Neil: Whose choice?

Vik: Mine. Also hers. But mostly mine.

Neil: Uh-huh.

Vik: Look, my weekends are about discipline. I wake up at 6. Do fasted cardio. Then I—

Neil: —spend 8 hours reorganizing your cable drawer?

Vik: First of all, it's a *cable management system*. Second, yes.

Neil: Okay, enough about your lonely Batcave. Send me that report.

Vik: Sending. And Neil?

Neil: Yeah?

Vik: Don't tell anyone I mentioned "Bridgerton."

Neil: Already in the group chat.

Vik: ...I hate you.

Neil: You'll get over it. You are vengence, right?

Vik: Don't push it, Mehta.

[Private Teams Chat – Neil <> Reya – 10:26 AM]

Reya: Did you see Sid's update? He suddenly needs "an extra day"? Feels like he's building himself an alibi.

Neil: Oh, I've got something better than a feeling. Just spoke to Vik.

Reya: Please tell me you didn't flirt your way into IT privileges again.

Neil: First, rude. Second, no—Vik owes me after I taught him how to use Excel without crying. Anyway... Sid's login activity from the night of the murder? Not from home.

Reya: Go on.

Neil: He was logged in using his phone's hotspot. Location pinged from Mumbai... facing the beach.

Reya: Facing the *beach*? What is this, a murder mystery or a dating show?

Neil: Could be both. Also, the GPS location is basically next to a "Sea Breeze Couples Retreat" motel.

Reya: Oh my god.

Neil: Yeah. Either he was avoiding home IP logs or... let's just say he wasn't there for the seafood platter.

Reya: And this is the same guy who claimed he just "went home"?

Neil: Yep.

Reya: Wow. This man's survival instincts are made of bubble wrap.

Neil: Exactly. And remember, he's also the one who tried to float the "Sonia was suicidal" narrative—except Jay denied it, and Sam contradicted him.

Reya: Bingo. It's all noise. They're trying to rewrite her story after she's gone.

Neil: Or cover their own.

Reya: Or both. I'm telling you, Sid's hiding something.

Neil: I'll ask him where he was that night. You just play along.

Reya: Wow. If you're gonna do that, please *don't* lead with "So, the murder." Maybe ease into it. Otherwise... don't. We'll find another way.

Neil: Copy. But if he says "hotspot" before I do, I'm buying myself cake.

[Microsoft Teams Chat – (Project Quantum Flow) Sid, Reya, Neil – 10:05 AM]

Sid: Hey Reya, Neil—hope you both had a restful weekend.

Reya: Lol define restful.

I saw my dad, argued about my career, then meal-prepped through emotional exhaustion.

Neil: I slept in, watched Formula 1 clips for 3 hours, then questioned my own productivity. 10/10.

Sid: Great. Because we're kicking off a quick sprint. I'll loop you in on a UI revamp task, Neil. Reya's already on the branding part.

Neil: OMG finally! I've heard about "working with Sid" like it's a rite of passage. Can't believe it's happening.

Reya: That's what I said before he sent me six versions of a logo brief at 3 AM.

Sid: I call it iterative empowerment.

Neil: Sounds like Stockholm Syndrome in Figma.

Sid: It's effective though.

Neil: Soooo... speaking of weekends... just curious—Sid, where *were* you the night Sonia... you know.

Sid: You mean... the night she passed away?

Neil: Yeah. I mean, not *incriminatingly*, just... as a citizen who also opens Google Calendar and wonders how people manage time.

Reya: Wow that was smoother than a porcupine in a balloon factory. Real smooth.

Sid: Uh... I dropped off my smartcard at her place. She needed access for a deadline.

Neil: That's so... helpful of you.

Sid: It was late. Around 9 PM. I left after five minutes. As I told to the Police as well.

Reya: and...

Sid: I left it on her desk and left.

Neil: So you're saying the ghost of Sonia opened the laptop, popped it in, and it automatically became Dev's.

Sid: ...I'm saying i gave her my smart card access and left, I have no idea what she did with my smart card or replaced it with Dev's

Reya: Let's maybe circle back to the UI work.

Neil: Right. Murder aside, can't wait to work with you both 😅

Sid: Murder aside, let's aim for Tuesday EOD.

Neil: So Sid... just circling back to that whole "left Sonia's apartment" thing. Where'd you go after?

Sid: Bro, not this again. We have a UI handoff due Thursday.

Reya: We can multitask.

Neil: Design critique *and* murder probe. It's the 2025 way. You said you left Sonia's around 9 PM. Where to?

Sid: Home.

Reya: Vik confirmed your log in near the beach, using your ow

Neil: That pause was suspicious.

Sid: ...Ish.

Reya: Ish?

Sid: Okay, not home.

Neil: Love the vagueness. Really inspiring confidence.

Sid: I wanted to get a drink, but all the places were closed, so I went to... uh... a friend's place.

Reya: "Friend's place" is alibi code for "definitely not innocent."

Neil: Yeah, that's one confession away from becoming a Netflix doc thumbnail.

Sid: I'm not a killer, okay?! I just... didn't want to say where because it's... embarrassing.

Reya: Oh my god, was it karaoke? Tell me it was karaoke.

Sid: Worse.

Neil: Escape room? Goat yoga?

Sid: Worse.

Reya: Sid, we're out of "worse" things.

Sid: Fine. After I left Sonia's, I went to a... sensory deprivation tank session.

Neil: ...

Reya: ...

Neil: Bro.

Reya: BRO.

Sid: What? I'd booked it weeks ago!

Reya: She literally called you before deleting herself!

Sid: IK and I still regret that!

Neil: So, you were floating in pitch-black saltwater like a human pickle... while your colleague was dying?

Sid: I didn't *know* she was dying! It's for stress relief!

Reya: You couldn't just... meditate? With your phone on your side for once!

Sid: No, because the spa has this "deep silence" thing where they take your phone. That's why I didn't answer calls for hours.

Neil: Oh, that's *so* suspicious. "Sorry officer, I was naked in a pod like a brined cucumber."

Reya: And you paid for this?

Sid: Yes! They give you herbal tea after!

Neil: So, you left a potential crime scene to... go marinate yourself.

Sid: It sounds worse when you say it like that.

Reya: Screenshots or it didn't happen.

Sid: Sending. *[Shares spa booking confirmation, timestamped check-in photo of his feet in disposable slippers]*

Neil: Oh my god, this is real.

Reya: Yep. The only thing you're guilty of is poor decision-making and being too pruney for your own good.

Sid: So... we're good?

Neil: Morally? No. Legally? Yeah.

Reya: You're not the killer—just someone with terrible taste in relaxation methods.

Sid: Thank you.

Neil: Also, you're never living this down. At the Diwali party, I'm introducing you as "the float tank guy."

Reya: I'm making bingo cards. "Sid was marinating during the murder" is the free square.

Sid: I deserve that. But seriously—this stays here.

Neil: Case closed. Now, back to the sprint.

Reya: And the murder.

Sid: Both equally terrifying.

[Private WhatsApp – Neil<> Reya 6:16 PM]

Neil: So...
Was that real life or the pilot episode of some low-budget Netflix thriller?

Reya: I'm still recovering from "he was at a beachside couples' motel for spa."
Sir... this isn't Love Island. You lead the UI team.

Neil: I swear, every time I think Sid's just a chill boring guy who says "synergy" too much, he drops something like this.
Imagine if HR had to file that in an official report.

Reya: *"Suspect unavailable for questioning due to floating like a human pickle."* 💀💀💀

Neil: They'd need a whole new crime category: "Murder... but spa day."

Reya: And the fact he *paid* for this? Peak suspicious-but-legal energy.

Neil: Exactly. Like, you're telling me you left a potential crime scene to marinate in the dark while listening to whale noises?

Reya: To be fair, he did have a booking confirmation. I saw the timestamp.

Neil: Yeah, but he could have pre-booked *anything*. Skydiving. Goat yoga. Professional clown seminar.

Reya: Goat yoga would have been less weird.

Neil: Honestly, it's the perfect alibi. "Sorry officer, couldn't have killed her, I was seasoning myself."

Reya: Ugh. I hate that we technically have to clear him now. Feels like we're... circling.

Neil: You think he's completely innocent though?

Reya: Of murder? Yeah. Of being an emotional disaster? Absolutely not.

Neil: We'll find out. One bizarre weekend hobby at a time.

Reya: You're cute when you're determined.

Neil: You're cute when you're suspicious of men.

Reya: That's just called experience.

Neil: Damn. Fair.

Reya: Okay. Let's circle back tomorrow. If I spiral now, I won't sleep.

Neil: Goodnight, gravity. You keep me grounded even when I'm spinning.

Reya: You're lucky you're cute.

How Nurobit Employees Contribute to Solving a Murder

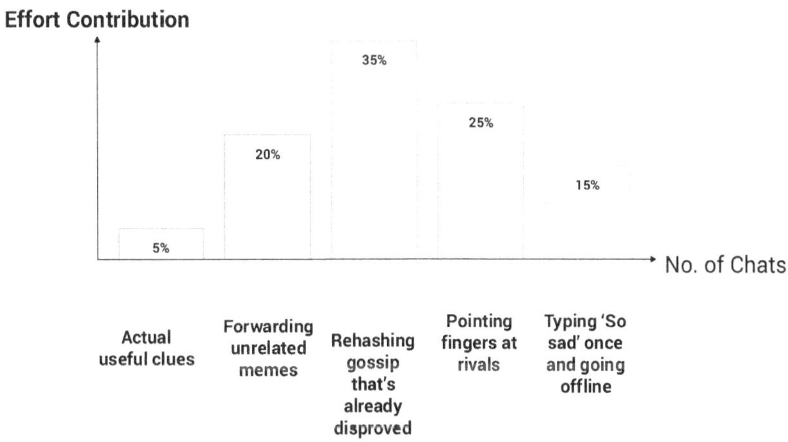

CHAPTER 09

To CC or Not to CC

[Microsoft Teams – #design-strategy – 09:25 AM]

CJ: Good morning team. Check the mails, do the needful.

Dev: Sonia's tasks are being redistributed. Maya, please review Dia's report. Neil and Aerron, follow up with Sid's access logs today.

Sid: Noted.

Maya: On it.

Sahil: Guess who's starting his day with a thrilling Excel deep dive?

Mini: Good morning all :)

Vik: Morning.

Ritika: Good morning team!

Amaan: Good morning!

Neil: Morning team

Vik: Good morning

[Private teams Chat – Vik <> Neil]

Vik: Yo. Got Sonia's laptop back.

Neil: Wait—*her* laptop-laptop?

Vik: Yep. The one IT confiscated. Forensics finally cleared it.

Neil: Tell me there's a trail of clues leading straight to the killer.

Vik: Bro. It's so anticlimactic.

Neil: Don't say she left a PowerPoint with "Things I Hate About Dev."

Vik: I *wish*.

It's mostly work stuff. Static. Routine. One master folder labeled "WIP – March."

Neil: Damn. Even her chaos was organized.

Vik: I swear she had version control for her emotions.

Neil: LMAO accurate.

Vik: There's one Excel sheet under personal folder.

Named "Feb Budget – Groceries."

Neil: Omg.

Vik: Bro she had macros for dal.

Neil: Of course she did.

Vik: One tab for "necessary veg," another for "emotionally necessary veg."

Neil: She would absolutely classify avocados as a financial threat.

Vik: Anyway, I peeked at her browser history. Nothing criminal.

Mostly work links, couple IG story logins, and a LOT of jewelry sites.

CaratLane, Tanishq, even those sketchy ads that say "5 rings under ₹999."

Neil: Could be window shopping. Or looking for a gift?

Vik: My guess is gift. Found a folder named "Dad – 25th Anniv."

Had screenshots of bands with "Forever annoyingly yours" engraved.

Neil: That's weirdly sweet.

Vik: Yeah, hit me right in the Ctrl+S.

Neil: So nothing weird. No private files? No secret diaries?

Vik: Unless "UI Review Notes v5_FINAL2" counts as scandalous.

Neil: Depends. Did it involve Comic Sans?

Vik: Wait—there was *one* thing.

Neil: 👀

Vik: Her lock screen wallpaper.

Neil: Okay??

Vik: It's a selfie. Her smiling. But there's a guy in the background.

Half his face is out of frame, but he's got his arm on her shoulder.

Neil: Face visible?

Vik: Nope. Just... half a jawline and his hand. But—

Neil: But?

Vik: He's wearing a fancy watch. Leather strap. Glass cracked. Looked... expensive.

Neil: Huh.

Vik: You know anyone who wears one like that?

Neil: ...Possibly.

Vik: You okay?

Neil: Just had a moment.

Vik: Should I send you the pic?

Neil: Yeah. Send. Please.

Vik: Done. You tell me if it's something.

Neil: Trust me. I think it is.

[Microsoft Teams – Dev:lopers (Dev, Aerron, Neil)– 05:16 AM]

Neil: Yo quick question.

Aerron: Here we go.

Dev: What did I do now 😩

Neil: Remember that birthday watch we got Dev? What model was it again?

Aerron: Ah yes. The *Tissot PRX* , aka the "Cursed Edition."

Dev: LOL don't start

Neil: Wait. Why cursed?

Aerron: Because I "tested" it before gifting it. Slipped on my bathroom mat like a Marvel stunt double. Scratched the dial. Boom. Instant depreciation.

Neil: LMAOOO

Dev: He fell *twice*, btw.

Aerron:I gave it *character*. That scratch is our *bonding scar*.

Dev: You mean my permanent reminder that my most trusted buddy in the office has zero balance.

Neil: So... Dev. You still have it, right?

Dev: Obviously. That watch is my *prized possession*. I wear it only on special days.

Aerron: Yeah, I've barely seen it in office.

Neil: True. You wear your Fitbit like a prediabetic dad.

Dev: Gotta track those 11 PM stress walks somehow.

Neil: But real talk—what counts as a "special occasion"?

Dev: Idk. Birthdays. Anniversaries. Big weekends. Stuff like that.

Neil: So like... birthdays?

Dev: Yeah. That's what I said.

Neil: Sonia's birthday?

Dev: ...what do you mean.

Neil: Sending something. One sec.

[Neil sends image: Sonia's laptop wallpaper – blurry selfie, arm around her, *watch with visible scratch*]

Aerron: WAIT.WAIT WAIT WAIT IS THAT— IS THAT THE WATCH??

Neil: Same model. Same leather band. *Same scratch*

Aerron: Bro I literally see the chip near the 2 o'clock mark. That's *your* scar. Dev.

Neil: Say something.

Dev:...Where did you get this?

Neil: Vik pulled it from Sonia's laptop.

Aerron: Bro. Were you—

Neil: Sonia's boyfriend.

Aerron: Bro

Neil: Secretly

Aerron: BROO

Neil: You gonna explain?

Aerron: Or you just gonna sit there ghosting like it's Sonia all over again?

Dev: Okay. Fine. You want the truth?

Dev: I broke up with Aditi . LDR wasn't working. She was busy, I was tired. It felt... dead. And then Sonia and I started spending more time together—late nights, meetings, walks after office. It just happened. Casual. I didn't mean for it to be a thing.

Neil: A *thing*? She literally had you on her wallpaper.

Aerron: That's not casual, bro. That's lock screen commitment.

Dev: I didn't know she set that photo. I never asked her to. She knew it was... not going to last.

Neil: Did she? Did you *actually* say that out loud or just vibe it into the universe and hope she'd get the memo?

Dev: I told her I was confused.

That it was a rebound.

She said she was okay with it.

But over time... she caught feelings.

Started asking if we were exclusive.

Started talking like... it was real.

Aerron: And you?

Dev: I panicked.

And my ex texted me out of nowhere last month. Said she was coming back.

Suddenly I had to choose.

And I didn't want to lose my ex—not for something I didn't even understand with Sonia.

Neil: So you dropped her.

After breadcrumbing her for weeks.

Dev: I tried to end it gently.

We met last Sunday. I told her it was over.

She was quiet. Cold.

Didn't say much.

I thought she was mad. But not... this.

Aerron: You don't get to be surprised.

You played her.

Neil: She *trusted* you. You were her senior, her friend.

You knew she'd already been burned by Devs like you.

Dev: It wasn't supposed to go this far.

I didn't think...

I didn't think she'd take it this hard.

Neil: You didn't think, period.

Aerron: I'm not saying you killed her.

But you *broke* her, man. And now she's gone.

What in the end it really was a suicide? And all because of you.

Dev: ...wish I could go back. I really do.

Neil: Too late. Although im sure its not a suicide.

[Private WhatsApp Chat – Neil <> Reya – 11:11PM]

Neil: Hey love. You up?

Reya: Yep. Still processing my last call where the client said, "Can we make the logo... *less opinionated*?"

Neil: LMAO. They just want Helvetica and silence.

Reya: Correct. So what's the drama? I saw Aerron post "Dev you snake" on Twitter.

Neil: Oh you're not ready.

Reya: I was born ready. Spill.

Neil: Dev confessed.

He was Sonia's secret boyfriend.

Reya: WHAT.

Neil: Yup.

Started dating her after breaking up with his LDR girlfriend. Called it a rebound.

Said it was casual.

But Sonia caught feelings.

Then and now his LDR ex-came back and he ghosted Sonia.

Reya: This man just speed ran "How to emotionally destroy a woman in three weeks."

Neil: He really went "thanks for the comfort, now please disappear."

Reya: So Sonia got dumped and ghosted by the same guy she trusted at work?

No wonder she looked like she was holding back a storm every time someone said "deadline."

Neil: Honestly... I feel sick.

He kept saying "it wasn't serious."

Like that makes it better.

Reya: That's Dev's brand. Emotional negligence with a beard.

Neil: Aerron and I backed him into a corner with the watch.

Reya: Wait, *the* watch?

Neil: The Tissot we gave him—the one Aerron "accidentally customized" by falling on it?

That scratch showed up in Sonia's wallpaper photo.

Reya: STOPPPP that's so niche and poetic I could cry.

Neil: I know. Sherlock would be proud.

Reya: I'm proud.

You really pieced it all together.

Neil: I just wish the truth made me feel better.

It doesn't.

Reya: Because it's not a win. It's a heartbreak in puzzle form.

Sonia deserved someone who didn't treat her like a placeholder.

Neil: Yeah.

And now she's gone.

And Dev gets to cry into his fitbit.

Reya: He'll be fine. Guys like him always are.

It's the Sonias of the world who get buried too soon.

Neil: I miss her.

Reya: Me too.

Want a voice note to sleep to? I can recite client feedback like bedtime horror.

Neil: Please do.

Also remind me never to become the kind of guy who says "it wasn't serious."

Reya: You're safe. You send good morning memes and ask about my migraines.

Neil: That's true love.

Reya: That's premium boyfriend tier.

Now rest, Detective Mehta. You've earned it.

Neil: Goodnight, Watson.

Reya: Goodnight, Emotional Literacy King.

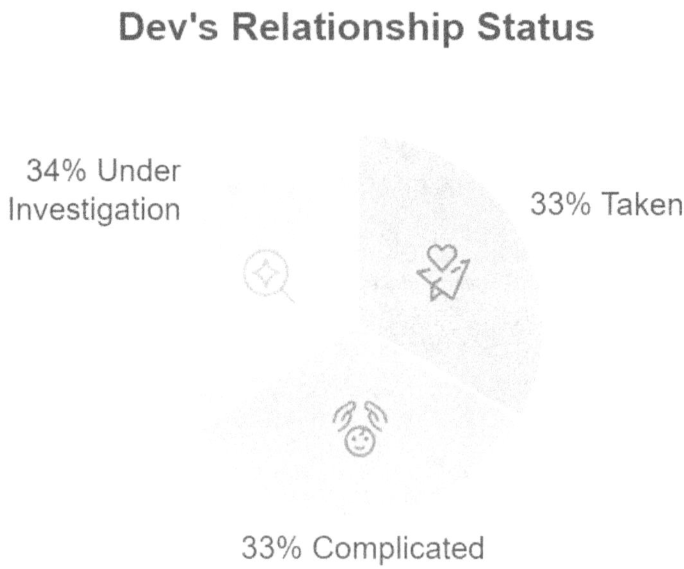

Chapter 10

FINGER GUNS AND ROSES

Dear Team,

The police have concluded their investigation into Sonia Arora's passing. Due to lack of evidence, the case has been officially ruled a suicide.

This has been a difficult time for all of us. Sonia was sharp, passionate, and famously opinionated about font choices — a presence we'll truly miss.

As a small gesture, HR will be putting together a PowerPoint tribute to share at Friday's all-hands. If you have any photos, screenshots, or kind memories involving Sonia (work-appropriate, please), kindly send them to **tribute@nurobit.corp** by Thursday 5 PM.

We understand this may be emotional. If you'd prefer not to attend, feel free to opt out via the HR portal under "Grief Preferences."

Thank you for handling this with compassion — and yes, we know a PowerPoint can't capture a whole person, but we're trying.

Warmly,

HR

Head – People & Culture

Nurobit Solutions

[Microsoft Teams – #design-strategy – 10:15 AM]

CJ: Good morning, team. Please remember to log your hours accurately this week. Thanks.

Dev: Neil, Aerron – can you both sync on the UI refinements before tomorrow's review?

Neil: Yep, will ping Aerron after lunch.

Sid: Dia, Maya – check the audit trail Sonia left. I need a cleaned-up folder structure by EOD.

Maya: Got it.

Dia: Sure.

Mini: Morning!

Maya: Morning :)

Jay: Hello everyone.

Sid: Dev, Dia — can you share the updated UI deck from Sonia's files?

Dia: Sure. Just extracting some folders now.

Dev: Working on it. Might take a while, her naming system is chaos.

Aerron: Why is there a folder called "Final_Final_ThisOneFr"?

Dia: That's nothing. I found one named "useThisMaybeLOL".

Neil: I'm surprised there isn't a "DoNotOpen_ExceptIfDeadline".

Sid: On a serious note — let's finish what she started. We owe her that much.

Dia: Agreed.

Rishab : Do we keep her old layouts or try new ones?

Dev: Preserve the good stuff, rework where needed. Sonia was always 3 steps ahead on UI flow — follow her lead.

[Private Teams Chat – "LOW-LIVES" – 10:51 PM] *(Members: Neil, Reya, Dia, Maya, Sam, Jay, Aerron, Mini, Rishab, Vik, Ritika, Amaan, Sahil)*

Sam: You guys saw the update?

Reya: Yeah.

Dia: ...officially ruled a suicide.

Amaan: What bullshit.

Ritika: They said "lack of evidence." But we *know*. We *know* she didn't do that to herself.

Vik: I've worked in IT long enough to know what deleting a browser history *too well* looks like.

Neil: And that laptop was *chemically wiped*, man. Who does that? Dexter?

Sahil: Sorry, but like... what even *is* chemical wiping? Is it like sanitizing with chlorine?

Aerron: It's like bleaching your ex's hoodie, but for data.

Dia: This isn't funny.

Mini: It really isn't. We failed her.

Reya: We all did. We couldn't even give her justice.

Neil: She deserved more than... a company-wide grief workshop and a closed case file.

Jay: I don't even think she liked me. But damn. No one deserves to go like that.

Vik: She *definitely* didn't like you, bro. Everyone could see she was ignoring you.

Ritika: so in the end it was all just stupid anxiety that took our youngest and brightest.

Maya: could be, mental illness can have many symptoms. depression or anxiety.

Neil: Regardless of that I think among us it has been established that she didn't off herself. I don't know what happened. It's just she is not with us anymore.

Aerron: Can we just... say something about her? A memory? Something good?

Maya: Okay. Once she caught me crying in the server room and pretended, she came in to "fight the server" for overheating. She smacked it with a ruler and made it beep.

Dia: She used to schedule emails with subject lines like "Sonia's Not Dead (Yet)" when she'd call in sick. I found one in my inbox two weeks ago and just stared at it.

Mini: She told my dad I deserved a raise before I even said a word. Said I had "main character intern energy."

Ritika: She told me never to date a guy who uses Comic Sans ironically.

Vik: She once bribed me with hot chocolate to "accidentally crash the VPN" during a client meeting. She paid in advance.

Reya: She sent me a meme during my first week here that said: "Welcome to corporate. We cry in slides now."

Neil: She mocked me for wearing a hoodie in 32°C. Said I looked like a budget Assassin's Creed NPC.

Jay: She threatened to replace my mouse with a rock and say it was "ergonomic."

Sam: ...Can I say something?

Neil: Please do, as long as it's not another confession.

Sam: No no, just... something I never told anyone. I think Sonia was dating Dev.

Dia: WHAT?

Reya: Back up. What?

Sam: I saw her texting someone with a saved contact name that just had a "D" and a black heart. I asked her—half-joking—if it was Dev. She gave me this *look* and said, "Does it matter?"

Mini: Doesn't he have a long distance girlfriend?

Vik: Wait wait wait. So Mr. Budget Engagement Ring *was* cheating?

Maya: This is getting so good and so awful.

Aerron: They were on a break or something.

Sahil: so Mr associate was associated with 2 others?

Rishab: what does that mean Sahil?

Sahil: Dev and Sonia were sleeping around.

Ritika: mind you intern Rishab is just 17 please don't use words like sex in front of him. Use code instead, in case HR sees this chat.

Sahil: I wasn't going to

Rishab: guys I know what sex is.

Reya: I think we are loosing the plot here.

Sam: How can she even do this to me? I mean us?

Neil: We never really knew her. Not all of her.

Maya: But we *felt* her. And that has to count for something.

Aerron: I just miss her sarcasm, man. The group chat has been way too well-behaved lately.

Dia: She'd probably call this group "Collective Failure" and mute us forever.

Neil: Honestly? Deserved.

Sam: I just hope she knows we tried.

Reya: She knew. I think... she knew we loved her. In our own broken, stupid ways.

Jay: And that's the most wholesome thing I've ever heard in a group named "WTF is this group?"

Aerron: Okay wait—can we *chill* on the Dev slander for a sec?

Neil: Yeah. Look, what he did with Sonia? Not cool. But his alibi checks out. Vik confirmed his smartcard wasn't even logged in *after* Sonia's death.

Vik: Facts. The card was cloned.

It got popped in for like 30 seconds, no login, no activity. Classic amateur framing.

Jay: Dev got framed AND dumped?? My man's living in an episode of *Suits* written by interns.

Reya: He breadcrumbed Sonia for months and *still* managed to look like a confused golden retriever in his police interview.

Rishab: Wis breadcrumbing code for sex?

Maya: To be fair, he did cry in the elevator. For six floors straight.

Amaan: Yeah but that could've just been the air freshener. It's *intense.*

Mini: Or guilt. Or Axe body spray. Same thing these days.

Rishab: Can we talk about how Dev wore a *white linen shirt* to the office the day after Sonia died? Like it was a *resort brunch*??

Sahil: That man grieves like a Goa pre-wedding photographer.

Neil: Okay okay. Roasting aside—he's not a killer. He was just... emotionally unavailable with romantic side quests.

Sam: Sonia deserved better than a side quest.

Reya: She *was* the main story. He just didn't know it.

Aerron: Yeah. He messed up. But he's not the one who killed her.

Jay: I still vote we key his new car for spiritual closure.

Maya: I second this.

Ritika: Let's just be real—we're not going to get justice. Not the kind she deserved.

Amaan: But we *can* remember her.

Talk about her. Keep her real, even if the system won't.

Mini: And tell Dev to stop doing sad-boy Zoom calls from his balcony with the ocean filter on.

Sahil: It's like watching a breakup reel in 480p.

Vik: Also... did anyone else notice he started using #healing in his captions?

Neil: We can't fix what happened. But we can at least stop pretending everything's fine.

Reya: Yeah. Let's not let it become just another line in a quarterly HR report.

Sam: "One (1) employee ceased to be." 😓

Maya: Ugh.

Reya: I miss her.

Ritika: Same.

Neil: Still think she'd haunt us just to say, "Y'all are idiots."

Sahil: She'd be right.

Aerron: But at least we're her idiots.

Sahil: And that's something, isn't it?

Reya: It is.

Vik: So... are we still keying Dev's SUV or what?

Jay: Oh 100%. Group activity. We bond, we heal.

Neil: Emotional closure through petty vandalism. Sonia would approve.

Rishab: is vandalism code for sex?

[Private WhatsApp Chat – Neil <> Reya – 4:17PM]

Neil: okay. group chat today was... a lot.

Reya: yeah. like a TED Talk but with trauma and memes.

Neil: accurate. ngl tho... it hit me harder than i expected.

everyone had something to say about her. something funny.

and yet it still feels like... we barely knew her.

Reya: we knew *parts* of her. the curated bits. the version she let us see.

Neil: yeah. and now that she's gone, i just keep wondering what i missed.

like maybe i should've asked her to grab coffee more. talked beyond the tasks.

Reya: or hugged her that one time she said she was "just tired" in that weird voice.

Neil: yep.

also can we talk about how dev got absolutely flamed by the entire team 😱😱

Reya: bro didn't even log in today. probably rage-uninstalled WhatsApp.

i swear if he posts one more "growth is painful" story i'm reporting him for spam.

Neil: "healing isn't linear"

caption over a latte and a cloud.

make it stop.

Reya: 💀💀💀

Neil: but real talk... i miss you.

not just us goofing off. like actually. i miss your face. your voice.

your weirdly judgemental eyebrows when i open 47 Chrome tabs.

Reya: aw shut up. i miss you too.

especially your chaos energy and inability to commit to a single water bottle.

like bro just hydrate. why are there THREE bottles on your desk.

Neil: hydration is a vibe not a process.

Reya: that is the dumbest thing I've heard and i will be using it forever.

Neil: trademark it pls.

Reya: already making merch.

Neil: but hey—actually—I had a thought.

I think I'm onto something, I'm going to call you in 10.

Reya: yeah sure. Care to elaborate?

Neil: will explain on the call, you might have to go pick up a drink for me from a place. Not the poison coffee type, I'll explain.

Reya: ...still not funny and waiting. I'll put on my shoes till then.

Where Everyone's Focus Actually Is

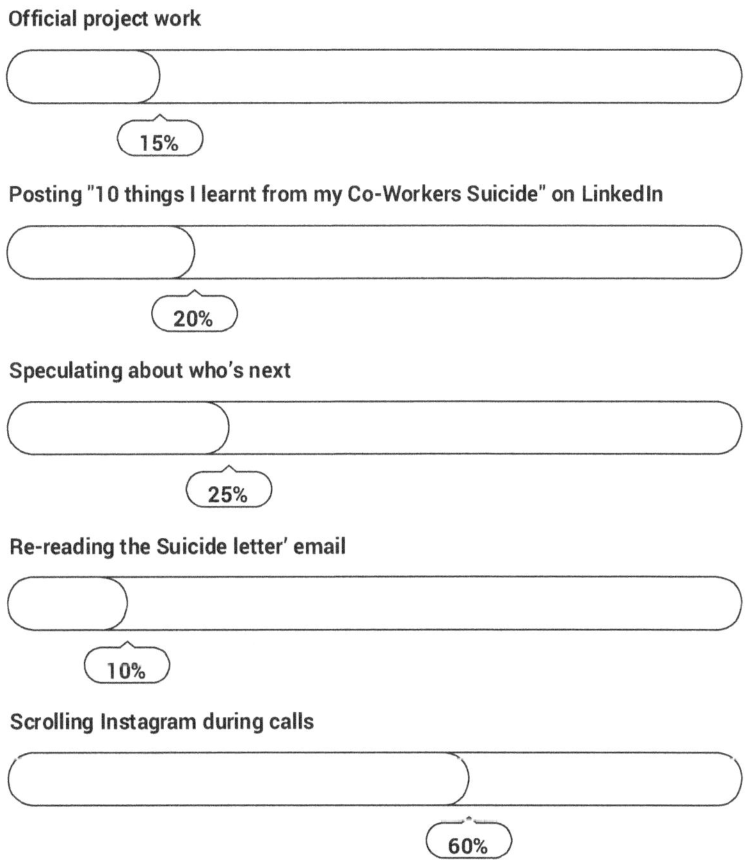

Chapter 11

THE WHOLE TRUTH AND NOTHING BUT THE TRUTH

[Microsoft Teams – #design-strategy – 09:25 AM]

CJ: Good morning people of neurobit -

Jay: Morning fam. Who's caffeinated and emotionally repressed today?

Reya: ✋ got oat milk and unresolved issues, I'm ready.

Sam: I slept 4 hours and dreamt about getting fired *at* a dream job. Does that cancel out?

Ritika: I spilled cold brew on my white shirt so we're already in villain arc territory.

Vik: Reminder: VPN's down for 15 mins for maintenance.

Also reminder: I didn't break it this time.

Amaan: Bold of you to assume we believe that.

CJ: I see the spirit is back!

Mini: Good morning team, let's kill this sprint!

(Just the sprint. Not each other. Been there.)

Aerron: LOL too soon bro.

Sahil: On a scale of 1 to "Sonia's ghost is haunting this thread," how cursed is today feeling?

Neil: about to make it a solid 11.

Reya: oh no.

Maya: what did you do.

Dia: please don't say it's code-related I don't have the strength.

Neil: not code.

murder.

Jay: wHAT

Neil: I know who killed Sonia.

Sam: HAHAHA okay cool so we're just doing *that* on a Tuesday morning?

Neil: dead serious.

Ritika: is this another metaphor? like "capitalism killed her"??

Neil: I mean, yes, but also—

I have receipts.

Reya: wait. wait. wait.

Maya: what kind of receipts are we talking? Amazon? iCloud? Crime?

Neil: digital. timestamps. deleted logs. accidental pings.

Vik helped.

Vik: I would like to be excluded from the murder narrative.

Amaan: bro are you saying what I think you're saying?

Neil: yes. I know who did it. I can prove it. I've cross-checked logs, scrubbed metadata, and someone slipped.

Sahil: someone in this chat?

Neil: ...maybe.

Jay: 😱 don't say "maybe" like that what is this *Knives Out* fanfiction??

Aerron: is this why you've been ignoring my memes??

Neil: justice > memes. but yes.

Ritika: wait, are we *safe*? like emotionally and otherwise?

Neil: emotionally? never. but the killer? oh they're about to get exposed.

Meeting link dropping in 5.

Sahil: Do we need popcorn or a lawyer?

Ritika: do I change shirts or is murder fine in coffee-stained linen?

Neil: keep the stain. Sonia would've laughed at the chaos.

Sid: Please tell me you're not bluffing, Neil.

Neil: I've never been this serious in my life.

Vik: bro said "good morning" then casually declared vengeance like Batman with Wi-Fi.

Neil:

Sonia meant different things to all of you.

To some—she was a friend.

To others—a lover.

To a few—a colleague, an ex, maybe even a rival.

But to someone in this room...

She was a threat.

And to the truth?

She was a **victim**.

That's all she ever became in the end.

Let's rewind.

Everyone here remembers Sid's alibi. He said he left Sonia's apartment early to go home. Gross. But believable.

And maybe he did. Maybe he wasn't there when she died.

But there's one person who can come uninvited, a friend for which Sonia will open the door, preferably from the office to help with the late-night deadline. Just the two of them.

Which means... **Dia had no reason to text, call, or message Sonia** before showing up.

No digital history. No trail. Nothing to suggest they ever met that night.

How... convenient.

Then came the lie that gave her away.

Dia told us she and Maya were drinking together at a bar the night of Sonia's death.

A casual alibi.

Too casual.

But here's the thing.

It was a dry day.

And the bar they claimed to be at? **Closed.**

Reya confirmed it. She actually *went* there.

Asked around. Showed photos.

The bartender laughed.

Said, "We were closed the whole damn day."

That's when it clicked.

Maya lied for Dia.

But Maya was *home* that night.

Vik confirmed it. Her office laptop pinged her home IP, logged in for a 3-hour working session.

So Maya wasn't at the crime scene.

Dia... was.

And who else knew Sonia's exact dosage of anxiety meds?

Who else convinced her to get on them in the first place?

Dia.

She showed up that night.

Brought coffee.

Probably smiled. Maybe even sat with her while she drank it.

One cup for her.

One cup for Sonia—laced with **crushed anxiety pills**.

And then... she waited.

Once Sonia was gone—

Dia opened her laptop.

Drafted a suicide email.

Scheduled it.

Wiped the keyboard clean with—

The nail polish remover.

Nice touch, by the way. Citrus scent.

Almost... respectful.

She left.

Slipped back into the night.

Back to her trusted friend

Maya

Who for some reason is IN on this!

Efficient.

And almost perfect.

But you forgot one thing, Dia.

Truth makes noise.

Even when you bury it.

It leaks.

And all I couldn't figure out—

is **why**?

You had it all.

A job. Friends. A team. Even... some version of love.

Why kill her? and why frame dev?

CJ: ...Neil. This is *not* the appropriate channel for—

Sahil: SHUT UP CJ, THIS IS CINEMA.

Sid: Why am *I* mentioned first??

Mini: Because you lied about going home, Mr. "Home...ish."

Vik: Honestly, Sid, if you're going to have a fake alibi, at least make it one people want to believe.

Sid: I hate all of you.

Reya: I told you he was hiding something.

Ritika: Can we circle back to "Dia crushed anxiety meds into coffee"? That's... creative? Disturbing? Both?

Amaan: Murder AND artisanal beverage prep. We stan multitasking. But this is another level.

Maya: ...Neil, this is not how I wanted my Wednesday to go.

Dev: Why is my name here? Why am I framed in this plot?

Sam: Because your smartcard was found in her laptop, genius.

Dev: That's *circumstantial*!

Sam: *Circumstantial* is what guilty people say.

CJ: I will remind everyone that this is a workplace group.

Mini: And I will remind you that HR ignored the nail polish remover clue.

Mr. Kapoor: Is this... about that police matter?

Neil: Yes, sir.

Mr. Kapoor: Then carry on.

Aerron: WHAT. The CEO just gave us permission to gossip about a murder.

Rishab: Pin this message.

Reya: Focus. Dia's the only one who knew the exact dosage of Sonia's meds.

Ritika: And the only one who made it sound like a wellness check while actually delivering a fatal latte.

Dia: This is insane.

Sam: And yet here we are.

Sid: I'd like it noted for the record that I am innocent.

Reya: The record says "Beachside float tank boy."

Sahil: LOL.

Maya: I just... don't like how easily you all believe this.

Neil: You lied for her, Maya. The bar was closed.

Sam: BRB buying popcorn for this murder TED Talk.

Mini: "Truth makes noise"? Neil, are you auditioning for a crime podcast?

Vik: I'm just impressed he remembered all those details but forgets his company given passwords every 3 weeks.

Ritika: ...wait, so Dia's the killer? Like, *killer* killer? Not "kills deadlines" killer?

Sahil: BRO.

Amaan: The citrus-scented nail polish remover detail??? I'm shook and also slightly impressed.

Mini: We need to focus on the "Maya was IN on this" part. Maya? Sweet, quiet Maya?

Maya: First of all, I'm right here.

Sam: Yeah and apparently also at a *fake bar* with *fake drinks*.

Reya: To be fair, the bar *was* closed. I checked. Got laughed at by the bartender.

Sahil: Imagine lying about a bar visit and getting caught because your PI is Reya with a photo album.

Aerron: I'm sorry, but "Truth makes noise" is still living rent-free in my head.

Vik: Same. Also, side note: this is the first Teams meeting where I'm genuinely awake.

Dia: This is ridiculous. You've all lost your minds.

Sam: Yeah, okay, "totally innocent person" talk.

Mini: So... when do we vote her off the island?

Neil: Guys, this isn't Survivor.

Jay: It is now.

Ritika: Imagine killing someone *and* framing Dev. That's overachieving.

Dev: I'm still processing the fact that I got framed with *nail polish remover*. I don't even own nail polish.

Sahil: You do now.

Reya: Focus, people.

Sam: Sorry, just—Dia, did you really bring coffee *and* poison? Like a homicidal Starbucks?

Aerron: Pumpkin Spice Manslaughter.

Maya: ...

Mini: That silence is louder than Neil's "truth" speech.

Neil: Thank you.

Vik: Not a compliment.

Sam: So when's the next episode dropping, Neil?

CJ: Please do not monetize a murder investigation.

Sam: Too late, I'm already designing merch.

Mr. Kapoor: Make sure the font is corporate-approved.

Neil: ...this company is unbelievable.

Dia: I think I have to consult my lawyer.

Sam: ...Okay *BUT* before you do that, can you just... say "I didn't do it" really convincingly?

Mini: Yeah, just to set the record straight once and for all.

Sid: Or at least explain why you *didn't* kill Sonia. You know, for closure.

CJ: Please do *not* answer that in a corporate chat.

Amaan: Oh, please. This is better than HR training modules.

Vik: Dia, lawyers are great, but you're missing a chance to clear your name *and* control the narrative.

Reya: Seriously. If you're innocent, denying it right now will at least slow down the meme-making.

Ritika: *Will it though?*

Aerron: No, but still, just say it.

Maya: You guys are treating this like it's some reality show.

Sam: It *is* now. Welcome to "Who Killed Sonia?" — streaming live on Microsoft Teams.

Dev: Dia, just explain. You've been friends with Sonia for years. Why would you even—?

Mini: —And if you *did* do it, at least give us the *why*. People respect honesty.

Sahil: Do they?

Amaan: No, but we'd respect the tea.

Mr. Kapoor: As your employer, I must say you are under no obligation to comment.

Neil: As your co-worker, I must say you *absolutely* should comment.

CJ: I'm begging you, Dia, *don't*.

Sam: I'm begging you, Dia, *do*.

Rishab: Yeah, blink twice in emojis if you did it.

Vik: 💀💀 — like that.

Reya: Dia, this is your moment to either clear your name... or give us the season finale twist.

Maya: No one is making this easier for her.

Mini: Murder never *is* easy, Maya.

Dia: ...You're all insane.

Neil: We know. Now talk.

Dia:

You want to know *why*?

You want the *real* story?

Fine.

I was supposed to be promoted last year.

I worked my ass off. Stayed late. Picked up other people's slack.

And then **Dev**—Mr. Golden Boy with his fake humility and startup pedigree— got it

He even smiled at me in the hallway after...

Mr. Kapoor gave *my* role to someone else.

Said it was "restructured."

Then bought croissants for the team like that made it okay.

You know what that felt like?

It felt like watching your own blood get siphoned into someone else's raise.

I told myself this year would be different.

That *this* year, I'd get what I earned.

But then came Sonia.

Perfect, chaotic, confident Sonia.

The kind of girl my dad would've actually been proud of.

My dad owns three companies.

He loves success.

He loves sons.

He tolerated daughters.

When I got hired here, he said,

"Don't call me unless you're VP before 30."

Every promotion I didn't get was another reason to not show up for Diwali.

To not answer my texts.

To say, "I told you, you're soft."

I wasn't soft.

I was just...

invisible.

Until Sonia.

She wasn't even trying.

Flirting with Dev. Ignoring Sam. Getting by on Charm and brilliance and sheer... *Sonia-ness.*

And they were going to promote her.

Again.

Over me.

I snapped.

I *broke*.

So I visited her that night.

I brought Sonia coffee.

Same cup I'd shared with her a dozen times before.

Only this time... I added a little more.

A few crushed pills.

Ones I knew she had a prescription for—because I'm the one who told her to get them.

She trusted me.

She *always* trusted me.

She drank it.

She smiled.

And then she didn't wake up.

I cleaned it up.

I wrote the email.

I scheduled it.

Then I went to Maya's place.

Not because I wanted to.

But because I needed an alibi.

Maya...

She's like my sister.

She didn't even ask for details.

Just said,

"If you need me... I'm here."

I told her the bar story.

She backed me without blinking.

She thought she was protecting me from a system that never protected girls like us.

And maybe she was.

But none of it matters now.

Because Sonia's gone.

And I did that.

I did it because I was tired of being the background.

Because my father will finally pick up the phone now.

But I still hear her laugh when I close my eyes.

And I don't know how to live with that.

Maya: You don't understand what Dia is to me.

When I was sixteen and bleeding in a hostel bathroom, she was the one who broke in and cleaned me up.

When I called her at 2 AM the night my mother relapsed, she *walked* five kilometers to reach me.

She covered for me when I stole Adderall to survive final year.

She lied to HR when I broke down mid-presentation.

So when she said,

"Please. I need you."

I didn't ask why.

I didn't care what Sonia did or didn't do.

Sonia was bright, brilliant, loud.

Girls like her always die young.

I just never thought she'd take Dia down with her.

I lied for love.

Not for justice.

And if I had to do it again?

...I'd ask for a cleaner lie.

Sam: WHAT.

Mini: Oh my god oh my god oh my god.

Vik: And she just *drops* it like a patch note update.

Reya: ...I'm actually shaking.

Ritika: You're admitting it? Here??

CJ: Alright. Everyone stop. This is no longer banter. This is now a matter for the authorities.

Mr. Kapoor: Agreed. I am informing the legal team immediately. Police will need to review all relevant evidence.

Neil: I'll compile everything. Chats, emails, timestamps. Everything I've collected so far will be packaged for the investigators.

Amaan: You've *been* collecting?

Neil: ...yes.

Sahil: That's equal parts terrifying and useful.

Maya: This is insane.

Sam: Insane is finding out your coworker is a killer *before* your morning stand-up.

CJ: Everyone, enough. No more speculation. No more accusations here. I'm instructing *all employees* to take tomorrow off.

Mini: Paid?

CJ: ...Yes, Mini. Paid.

CJ: Dia, you are to remain at home until contacted by the authorities. You will not access any company systems in the meantime.

Dia: Fine.

Mr. Kapoor: Let the process take its course. This chat is now closed to further discussion on this matter.

Aerron: Just to clarify—closed as in "no more messages" or closed as in "muted until Neil inevitably drops another bomb"?

CJ: *Closed.*

Neil: Copy that. Evidence folder coming your way.

Sam: I feel like we just finished Season 1.

Reya: No, Sam. This is still the pilot.

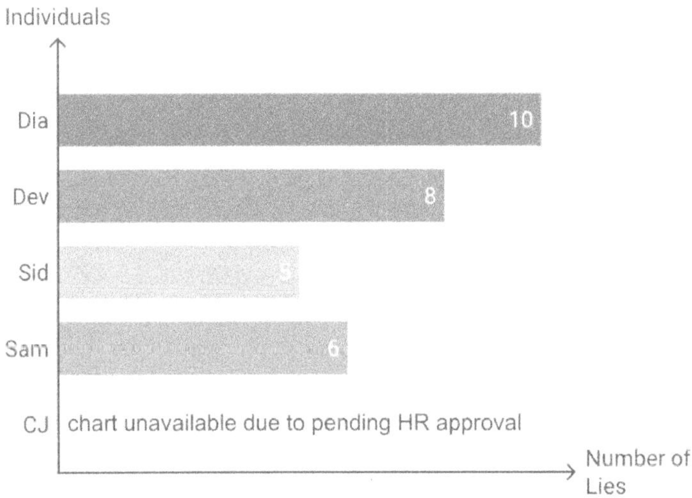

Frequency of Lies Told This Week

Chapter 12

SHOW OFF MUST GO ON

[Microsoft Teams – #design-strategy – 9:22 AM]

CJ: Good morning, everyone. Glad to see such a bright start to the day. We have *two* new joinees today—please welcome Rohit (Backend Developer) and Sanya (UI Intern).

Mini: Morning!

Sam: Morning, boss.

Mr. Kapoor: Morning, team.

Mini: Welcome!

Sam: Heyyy new people!

Amaan: Welcome!

Vik: Hi.

Ritika: Welcome aboard!

Reya: Welcome.

Neil: ...Hi.

Rohit: Thanks! Happy to be here.

Sanya: Excited to join the team!

Sam: Pro tip: Never reply to emails with "As discussed." It's a trap.

Mini: And avoid sitting next to Sid in stand-up meetings. He fidgets.

Sid: Wow, okay.

Aerron: Also, if CJ invites you for "a quick chat," block your calendar for at least an hour.

CJ: 😂 Let's be nice, team.

Mr. Kapoor: Let's make sure our new colleagues have all the support they need.

Reya: *[DM to Neil]* This is surreal.

Neil: *[DM back]* Like nothing ever happened.

CJ: Alright, let's get back to work. Rohit, Sanya—your onboarding sessions start at 11.

Sam: Oh, and don't Google the company name + "murder."

CJ: SAM.

Sam: Kidding! (Not kidding.)

[Private WhatsApp – Neil <> Reya – 10:42 PM]

Reya: Good morning, Sherlock. You actually found the killer.

Neil: *We* found the killer. Don't try to make me sound like some lone-wolf genius. You were the one who got the bartender to roast your alibi check.

Reya: Yeah, still can't believe my big contribution to justice was being laughed at by a man in an apron.

Neil: Hey, it worked. And thanks... for sticking with me through all of this.

Reya: Always. Even if it meant reading more Teams chat than any human should endure.

Neil: So, now everything's "back to normal." Maya was asked to quit quietly, Dev stepped down, and Aerron...

Reya: ...finally got the promotion by default. Honestly, that's the most anti-climactic ending to a murder subplot.

Neil: Yeah. And that's what's weirding me out. It hasn't even been a weekend since Dia was taken away, and the office already feels... fine. Too fine.

Reya: People move on. Or they pretend to.

Neil: Feels like pretending. Nobody's whispering in the pantry anymore. No one's awkwardly avoiding Sonia's desk. It's like she never existed.

Reya: That's corporate life. One person leaves, another takes their seat.

Neil: She died two weeks ago. It's not supposed to be this... I don't know what led to the end. But I do know she deserved more—more recognition, more kindness, more people who didn't flinch when she was loud, or broken, or honest.

Sonia was not easy to love. But she was worth loving.

And damn it, I miss her.

Reya: We all miss her but you know as they say *Show must go on.*

Neil: Yeah, but at what cost?

Reya: All of them. Always. That's the deal. We either get used to it, or it eats us alive.

Neil: You're right. Doesn't make it any less messed up.

Reya: Nope. But at least we know. And we cared enough to ask. That's more than most.

Neil: Guess that's our thing then. Caring enough to ask.

Reya: ...and sending each other memes about it after.

Neil: Deal.

[Private Teams Chat – Aerron <> Neil]
Neil: Got something in the mail today.
A letter. Handwritten. From Sonia.
Postmarked before she... you know.
It landed on my desk this morning.

Aerron: Damn. Really?
You okay?

Neil: Not really.
It's her handwriting.
You don't just... walk away from that.

Aerron: Want to talk? Or want me to break something until it feels better?

Neil: Maybe both.
Here—

---

neil,

happy belated birthday, you fossil. Didn't forget. Just... didn't want to text.
You once said handwritten notes are underrated. So here's one—don't you dare cry, or I'll haunt your fridge and swap your beers for buttermilk.

Thank you for being the only person here who never wanted anything from me. You made me feel like a person, not a performance.

I hope you and Reya get married soon. She's got that rare kind of softness that makes you want to be a better man. Don't lose that.

Also—yes, you were right. Jay still sucks.

I hope I get to see you happy. You deserve it.

—Sonia

Neil:
Feels like a goodbye letter from someone who didn't know she was saying goodbye.
Or maybe she did.

Aerron: And someone didn't let her change that ending.

Neil:
Yeah. And I can't fix hers.
But I can make mine count.
I'm going to propose to Reya. Not with a ring box in some overpriced restaurant—just... in person.
Something real. Something alive.

Aerron: LET'S GOOOOO. I'll run interference. Fake meetings. Fake client meltdown. Whatever you need.

[Private Teams Chat – HR <> Neil]
Neil: Need a few days off. Personal reasons.
CJ: Understood. Take them.

Nurobit Solutions Murder Investigation Cycle

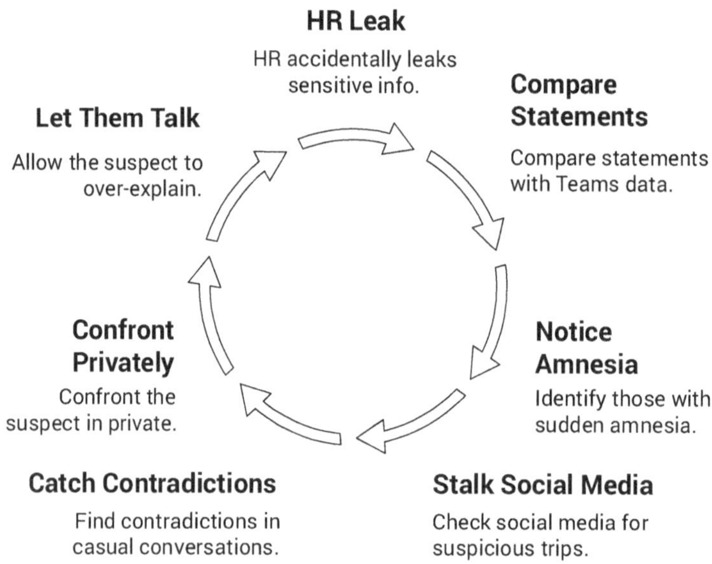

About The Author

This... is the day the world has been waiting for.

Every once in a while, a ***revolutionary book*** *comes along that changes everything. This is that book. With this breakthrough of a manuscript, the Author intends to prove that without art, the world is just commerce and science students wearing ill-fitting suits.*

The Author believes in the simple, not the complex... believes in changing the world — but never after billable hours. Speaking exclusively in the third person, the Author has mastered the art of saying "no" to thousands of projects, so they can focus on the precious few that are truly important, meaningful... and occasionally profitable.

Some books are written to dispense information. Others transport you to imaginary worlds. ***This book is neither.*** *This book is* *something more. At the Author's core — their core value — is the unshakable belief that people gossip all the time, and documenting that gossip with passion can change the world for the better.*

One of the ways the Author believes people express their appreciation to humanity is by making something wonderful... and putting it out there. So here it is. The gift. To you. You're welcome.

The Author politely requests that, upon finishing the book, readers should not feel compelled to give a standing ovation. A few slow claps will suffice.

Remember — this book is not here for your entertainment. ***It's here to change the world.***

www.ingramcontent.com/pod-product-compliance
Lightning Source LLC
Chambersburg PA
CBHW062142160726
48282CB00027B/904
9789334374032